Metaphysics

By the same author
Reason And Experience
An Introduction To Philosophy of History

Metaphysics

W. H. WALSH

A Harbinger Book

HARCOURT, BRACE & WORLD, INC.
New York

ISBN 0-15-659305-X

Library of Congress Catalog Card Number: 66-26470

Printed in the United States of America

D E

For

Everett and Cecilia Nelson

Preface

Some of the central arguments of this book were outlined in an essay of mine entitled 'True and False in Metaphysics', which appeared in the international number of *Filosofia* in November 1959. I have reproduced the actual wording of this essay in a few places. I have also used in Chapter 10 a passage from an earlier paper on 'Categories', published in *Kantstudien*, 1953–4. Chapter 9 is a revised version of a lecture I gave in the University of Toronto in 1958. I first had the leisure to try to work out my ideas about metaphysics in the academic year 1957–8, which I spent as a visiting professor in Ohio State University. I owe a deep debt of gratitude to Professor Everett J. Nelson, chairman of the Philosophy Department there, not only for inviting me, but also for the great generosity with which he treated me throughout my stay. I am also indebted to the University of Oxford and the governing body of Merton College, of which I was then a Fellow, for making it possible for me to accept the invitation.

Professor Paton read the typescript with his customary kindness and care, and made many suggestions for improving both the exposition and the argument, the great majority of which I have been happy to adopt. I take this opportunity to thank him for help and encouragement over many years.

Edinburgh   W.H.W.
November 1962

Contents

I

Introduction

THE very word 'metaphysics' is full of controversy; the emotions it excites vary in character, but are seldom anything but strong. There was a time when metaphysics was thought to be the highest form of knowledge, the most fundamental and comprehensive of all the branches of study to which human beings could devote themselves. Metaphysicians were said to be occupied with 'reality' as opposed to 'mere appearance', and they were supposed, as Plato put it, to take all being and all knowledge for their province. Because metaphysics was the fundamental discipline which discovered the most important of truths, its results might be expected to affect those of every other form of enquiry; the findings of all other sciences must accordingly be regarded as provisional, in need of revision or ratification by the metaphysician. It was to the metaphysician, again, that we must turn for enlightenment on those ever-present questions men asked themselves about the scheme of things entire: questions concerning the nature and origin of the universe as a whole, the nature and destiny of man, the existence of God. Metaphysicians not only undertook to pronounce on these subjects, but claimed to do so with peculiar certainty. For metaphysics was, its exponents said, a uniquely self-critical science; it was the only form of intellectual activity which left nothing unquestioned and proceeded entirely without assumptions. The only propositions with which a metaphysician could properly be content were propositions whose truth could not be denied, or whose truth was seen to be involved in their own attempted denial. To be 'in earnest with metaphysics', to use a phrase beloved of metaphysically minded Victorians, was accordingly seen as the highest of intellectual ambitions.

The prestige of metaphysics did not depend solely on the bold claims made on its behalf: it owed much also to the actual achievements of those who were described as metaphysicians. Plato and Aristotle among the ancients, Thomas Aquinas among the medievals, Descartes, Spinoza and Leibniz in the seventeenth century, even Hegel in the early nineteenth century, were on any estimate men of quite remarkable abilities. Others might have made more spectacular contributions in particular spheres—geometry, for example, or physics; what marked them off was the variety of fields to which they invited attention, the diversity of subjects on which they had illuminating things to say, and above all the combination of satisfying simplicity and promise of further application which characterized their theories. They each sought to produce a connected account of knowledge, and in each case the attempt proved positively useful as well as intellectually stimulating. Barriers between existing disciplines were broken down or challenged, fresh syntheses or groupings indicated. Thus the development of mathematics in the fourth century B.C. owed something to Plato's commitment to the 'synoptic' study he called 'dialectic', whilst the possibilities of the subject now known as mathematical physics were sketched for the first time in the *Timaeus*; the programme for a comprehensive account of natural phenomena, including living phenomena, in mechanical terms, which has proved so enormously influential in modern scientific investigations, was originally urged by Descartes as part of a large-scale metaphysical synthesis; the work of Hegel, long denounced for its barren apriorism, has turned out to be remarkable for its historical and sociological insights, and is having an effect on the growth of the social sciences which is certainly not diminishing at the present time. Proof that these writers still have something important to say to us is to be found in the fact that their works are extensively read and studied, as major works of literature are. The very fact that the ranks of metaphysicians have included men of this calibre would seem to be some ground for taking the large claims made for metaphysics seriously.

But whatever enthusiasm metaphysics may have aroused in its devotees it must be allowed that the reaction against it has been at least as violent, so violent indeed as to suggest that the issues involved in the controversy must be something more than academic. It was in the eighteenth century that the classical criticisms of the

claims of metaphysics were first developed by Hume and Kant, but
the subject had fallen into bad odour well before these criticisms
could be considered and digested. The term 'metaphysical' was
already pejorative for writers as diverse as Voltaire, Herder and
Burke. The motives behind the many attacks on metaphysics which
were developed by these and other thinkers of the period 1750–1850
were correspondingly various.

Thus Voltaire associated metaphysics with theology: the elimination of metaphysics was for him part of what was enjoined in the
celebrated slogan '*Écrasez l'infame*'. Burke and Herder, by contrast,
thought of metaphysics as the acme of *abstract* speculation; it was
in the name of empiricism, thought tied close to the realities of life,
that they denounced it. Hume wished to commit books of 'school
metaphysics' to the flames, 'as containing nothing but sophistry and
illusion', largely because of his antipathy to the claims metaphysicians like Descartes had made on behalf of human reason; to his way
of thinking the reason of man was no more competent to reach
ultimate truth than the reason of animals. This naturalistic outlook
was by no means shared by Kant, who protested against metaphysics
of the kind practised by his predecessors partly in the interests of
natural science, but more because of his ambition 'to abolish knowledge in order to make room for faith', which meant in effect to keep
the world safe for morals. To show up the pretensions of transcendent
metaphysics was essential if men were to be able to hang on to
certain fundamental beliefs, in God, the freedom of the will and the
immortality of the human soul, without which the moral life would
make no sense; speculative reason could provide no adequate
warrant for these beliefs, which must become matters of what Kant
called 'pure rational faith'. This is a view significantly different from
that of Kierkegaard, a slightly later critic of metaphysics, who also
opposed faith to reason but would certainly not have been satisfied
to describe his faith as 'purely rational', even if that term were
interpreted in the peculiar Kantian way. It was different again from
the position of Auguste Comte, in whose Positive Philosophy metaphysics was seen as an intermediate stage in an inevitable human
progress from animistic to scientific thought, a stage in which men
freed themselves of the illusion that all things are full of gods only
to set up a rival mythology of reified abstract forces. Metaphysics in

this account was something we must grow out of in order to attain intellectual maturity.

The period in which these attacks were being mounted was itself a time of renewed metaphysical activity. The successors of Kant, reacting against what they saw as the shallow materialism of the Enlightenment, and more conscious than their predecessors of the manifold activities of the human spirit, in art and literature, in religion, in the whole field of social life as well as in the pursuit of scientific knowledge, sought to construct fresh metaphysical syntheses which should take account of this diversity. Hegel in particular produced a system of striking power and originality, a system which, it is worth remarking, was still being imitated a hundred years after Hegel's death. (Whitehead might be described as an Hegelian at one remove.) But Hegel's intellectual pretensions were so vast, his style so barbarous and obscure and his explicit logic, so far as it could be discerned, so peculiar that hostile reaction to Hegelianism was intense. Baffled by the verbiage of the Hegelian system and affronted by what they took to be its author's cavalier attitude to empirical facts, critical philosophers were led into renewed denunciations of metaphysics.

A metaphysician, it was now argued, is the exact antithesis of a scientist: whereas the latter submits himself to the patient investigation of experience, taking the facts for what they are and accepting or rejecting theories as they accord with them or not, the metaphysician turns away from reality and constructs a fantasy world of his own. Unwilling to face unpleasant truths, he pretends that a different sort of reality underlies the obvious facts, a reality which is not accessible to the senses but whose nature can be established by pure thinking. The task of metaphysics is then to deal with what is *really* real, as opposed to empirically real. Yet how, the critics asked, could what metaphysicians said even be shown to make sense, let alone to be true, on this account of the matter? There were (the critics thought it obvious) only two kinds of significant statement: analytic statements which were true in virtue of the laws of logic and for that reason tautologous, and putative truths of fact which were meaningful in so far as they were capable of being checked against empirical evidence. Metaphysical statements could be put in neither category. They were clearly not analytic, since they professed to tell us something about the true nature of the world. But equally they could not pretend to the title of straightforward truths of fact, for metaphysicians notoriously despised the empirical world and had their eyes fixed on higher things. But if it was the case that nothing could count either for or against them, if metaphysical statements were, as they must be admitted to be, compatible with any empirical state of affairs whatsoever, then we must dismiss metaphysics as neither true nor false but 'literally senseless'. It was not denied that some metaphysical sentences might have an emotional effect, of the kind the critics associated with poetry (hymns or incantations might have made a better comparison); for weak minds metaphysics might certainly be meaningful in this non-literal sense. But nobody who had reflected could take its intellectual pretensions seriously for a moment.

Such, in summary outline, were the views of the Logical Positivists who flourished in Vienna in the 1920s and early 1930s and who sought to fashion, in their celebrated Verification Principle of Meaning, a weapon which would destroy metaphysics once and for all. The philosophers who adhered to the Logical Positivist movement were men with a conscious mission; many of them were scientists as well as philosophers, and 'Unified Science' was one of their principal watchwords. Their antipathy to metaphysics was like the antipathy of genuine practitioners to the lore of witch doctors; they abhorred it as senseless obscurantism. Whether they had ever examined it from close to is another matter, on which all that need be said now is that few of them showed much evidence of having done so. But, fair or unfair, the Positivist criticism of metaphysics had a tremendous effect on philosophical thinking in the years before and immediately after the 1939–45 war.

It is true that relatively few British and American philosophers were willing to enrol themselves under the banner of Unified Science, and again that difficulties were experienced from the first in producing a satisfactory formulation of the Verification Principle (and for that matter in justifying the sharp dichotomy of propositions into analytic and tautologous on the one hand and synthetic and putatively factual on the other). But whatever problems were encountered in stating and defending Positivist principles, the anti-metaphysical conclusions urged by the Positivists were very widely accepted. It became customary at this time to say that philosophy should not try any more to construct theories about the nature of the world as a whole, but should transform itself rather into a critical activity, concerned with the elucidation of the concepts of natural and social science. The major philosophers of the past were to be studied as analytic philosophers, not as metaphysicians.

Nor was the situation altered in any fundamental respect when the brief ascendency of the Logical Positivists came to an end and their place was taken by the so-called Linguistic Philosophers. The latter were, admittedly, committed to fewer dogmas than the Positivists; in particular, they felt no very strong urge to defend the cause of science. But if they had little inclination to repudiate metaphysics in the name of empiricism, the devotion to common sense which they had learnt from G. E. Moore made them no less hostile to the subject than the Positivists. It was characteristic of metaphysicians as these philosophers saw them to find difficulties, or even contradictions, in concepts of which we all make an everyday use; concepts such as *thing and property, relation, cause and effect, time, space, activity, change.* What we took to be obviously true, as for instance that the world in which we live contains a great number of material bodies, was declared by metaphysicians to be false; what was there was really a collection of monads, or a set of appearances of the Absolute. To followers of Moore paradoxes of this kind were evidently absurd: if philosophy found itself in conflict with common sense, it was clearly in the wrong. And their strong predisposition to dismiss metaphysics as misguided was reinforced when, thanks to the influence of Wittgenstein, the notion of common sense ceased to play a major part in their thinking and was replaced by talk about ordinary language. What we say in real-life contexts, as opposed to philosophical discussions, is all 'in order as it is', as is shown by the very fact that it is understood and acted on. A philosopher who questions the propriety of our everyday language can have no understanding of the many subtle distinctions we are able to make by using this language. He is, in a Burkeian sense (there are many similarities between Burke and Wittgenstein), committed to abstractions; and the only thing to do with him is to display to him the richness of what he is repudiating and the poverty of what he proposes to put in its place.

These remarks may suggest that metaphysics has been written off altogether by contemporary philosophers, in this country at least, but this is in fact not true. There has indeed been a distinct revival of interest in metaphysical writers and writings in the last few years, a revival manifested not only in renewed attention to philosophers like Plato, who were once dismissed as offering nothing but a combination of bad argument and distasteful uplift, but also in full-scale studies of individual metaphysical philosophers. Spinoza, Hegel and Bradley have each been the subject of monographs which are appreciative rather than critical; Aristotle and Leibniz enjoy more favour in professional circles than Locke and Hume; and the claims of Aquinas are being steadily pushed. It is true that the enthusiasm for metaphysicians is somewhat greater than that for metaphysical theories; the inclination is to say that the writer in question has interesting *aperçus* on particular points rather than to place a high value on his overall outlook. In the case of Aristotle, for instance, the tendency is to neglect the central doctrines of the *Metaphysics* and the articulation of the Aristotelian system as a whole in favour of a study of particular theories like that of the *Categories*; in a broad sense, it is the logical side of Aristotle's work which still attracts attention. But one may be permitted to wonder if this tendency will continue. A certain disenchantment with analytic philosophy, whose promise to deal with restricted problems piecemeal and in a scientific fashion has remained unfulfilled, together with an appreciation, derived from reflection on the case of Wittgenstein, of the importance of individual genius in philosophy, are among the factors which could conduce to a more full-blooded revival of interest in metaphysics. It would then be necessary to ask, once more, what metaphysicians are trying to do and what qualifications they have for carrying out the tasks in question.

I have written this book in the conviction that metaphysical literature has a fascination and an importance which have not been sufficiently appreciated by philosophers in Britain in the last half-century. I do not mean to imply by this that I regard the claims set out in my first paragraph above as one and all justified. As will become apparent, 'metaphysics' in my view is not the name of a single, simple activity; diverse metaphysicians have had diverse intellectual ambitions, and some of these seem, when viewed in perspective, altogether more respectable than others. But I should want to say that the theories of the great metaphysicians have a continuing interest in themselves as well as for the incidental light they throw on points discussed by analytic philosophers; despite all that has been said in criticism of them they deserve constantly renewed examination. To set them aside as 'literally senseless' is impossibly crude; to dismiss them as consisting of hopeless paradoxes, or seek to explain them away as reflecting the diseased minds of their authors, is scarcely better. We need to enter into the thought of a metaphysician as we enter into that of a writer of imaginative literature; we can derive enrichment and illumination from the first as much as from the second. A person who has succeeded in mastering the thought of a major metaphysician sees the world with fresh eyes; whether he accepts the point of view urged or not, the possibilities of experience have been multiplied for him. As in the parallel though also importantly different case of poetry, it will not do to set aside what is said here on the grounds that it is not the plain literal truth, or not what the scientist would tell us. What else it is if it is not the plain literal truth is of course another question, but one which can be discussed profitably only if we conduct the discussion with actual examples before us.

This brings me to the last point in these introductory remarks. The questions I shall be asking are the questions which were discussed a generation ago in the heyday of Logical Positivism, questions about the nature of metaphysical theories and their relation to experience, about the character and truth-conditions of metaphysical assertions and about the claims which metaphysicians have made to pass beyond the sensible world to the intelligible 'reality' which lies behind it. But I hope that in one respect at any rate the present discussion will break fresh ground. The anti-metaphysical polemics of the Positivists were conducted *in vacuo*, i.e. without reference to particular metaphysical writings; it was thought to be enough to quote an occasional sentence to illustrate the sort of nonsense with which the discussion was concerned. The effect of this was to turn the metaphysician into a man of straw; actual metaphysicians could and did say that the arguments adduced had nothing to do with them. We can avoid this unhappy result by keeping at least as close an eye on what metaphysicians have said as on what has been said about metaphysics. And we need to follow this policy if our discussion is to have any significance or interest for the modern student of philosophy, who has been brought up in an atmosphere which is predominantly anti-metaphysical and whose familiarity with the main classics of the subject is minimal. It is for this reason that I have chosen to begin with a short sketch of the philosophy of Plato, who, if not literally the first metaphysician, was the first man of genius to work at the subject and one of the greatest who ever took it up.

2

The Philosophy of Plato

1. *Knowledge and belief, with their practical implications*

A CONVENIENT point of entry into the thought of Plato is to see it as reflecting dissatisfaction with the state of knowledge achieved, and the claims to knowledge made, by Plato's contemporaries. At the end of the fifth book of the *Republic* Plato himself draws a contrast between two conditions of mind or 'capacities', to use his own term, to which he gives the names γνῶσις and δόξα, conventionally though somewhat misleadingly translated as 'knowledge' and 'belief'. The contrast is explained, in the first place, as a contrast in clarity: knowledge is a state in which everything is seen as it is and seen distinctly, belief one in which things are discerned dimly, seen as we see things in a dream. Believing as opposed to knowing, again, is said to be like seeing objects indirectly, by means of their shadows or reflections in water; the contrast here is with seeing them face to face and in a clear light. In the former set of conditions mistakes, and in particular the mistake of confusing one object with another, are all too likely to occur; in the latter they will not. It was Plato's conviction that ordinary men are in a state of belief throughout their lives; it was further his view that those who professed to teach them wisdom and understanding, the Sophists who thought that the secret of things would be yielded up if only we noted regular recurrences in experience, were themselves in no better case. Wisdom and understanding could come, according to Plato, only if men would abandon belief for knowledge, a process which would involve a violent break with past habits and ways of thinking, followed by a course of rigid intellectual discipline. In this way alone could they pass from acceptance of things as they appear to be, the condition of ordinary men and Sophists alike, to apprehension of things as they truly are, the condition of the true philosopher.

The passage from appearance to reality in this account is presented by Plato as if it were a transition from contemplating one class of entities to contemplating another, and this impression is confirmed by his characterization of belief and knowledge as 'capacities'. Every capacity, he tells us, is correlated with its own special object, that on which it is directed, with the result that there can be no question of the same things being believed and known. A partial explanation of this seemingly paradoxical view is to be found in the construction Plato put on the term 'knowledge'. Whereas knowledge and, still more, belief are to the modern mind primarily *about* something, Plato takes them as conditions in which, in each case, something is directly apprehended. The knowledge of which he speaks is thus Russell's 'knowledge by acquaintance' as opposed to his more familiar 'knowledge by description'; it is alleged to be illustrated, partially at least, by the situation in which we are said to know somebody, as distinct from knowing something about him. The model on which Plato (and for that matter Russell too) constructed his concept of knowledge is plainly that of sight: knowing is a superior sort of seeing, one in which an utterly stable object is discerned with infallible certainty. Plato's notion of knowledge as being thus intuitive has played an immense (and, some would add, a disastrous) part in the history of philosophy; our concern with it now is, however, only to point out that it provides the key to his concept of belief. For Plato construes believing too as if it were a sort of seeing, a seeing carried out in unfavourable conditions both as regards observer and observed, the former because illumination is poor and fitful, the latter because there is nothing steady about what is seen. Belief taken in this way clearly has an object of its own, just as knowledge has when considered as intuitive, and in each case mental state and object correspond exactly. To know is necessarily to know something, to believe necessarily to believe something, and the somethings cannot coincide, just because knowing and believing are distinct.

Plato distinguishes between the objects of knowledge and those of belief in various connected ways. One point he particularly stresses is that the former are just what they seem to be, which the latter conspicuously are not. The things we meet with in everyday experience, the 'many beautifuls' or the 'many just things', to give Plato's own examples, have the disturbing characteristic of manifesting opposite qualities. Each of the many beautifuls is beautiful, but equally each of them lacks beauty. By contrast 'the beautiful itself', the Form of Beauty which is an object of knowledge, always lives up to its pretensions: to suppose that *it* might not be beautiful is like supposing that the standard metre might not be a metre long.

Plato's reasons for thinking that the many beautifuls cannot be genuinely beautiful but must on the contrary be defective in truth and reality (ideas which are both implied in his single word ἀλήθεια), are not as clear as we might hope. He says more than once in the *Phaedo* and the *Republic* that the objects of sense-perception, which form a conspicuous part of the objects of belief, are subject to constant change; his elaboration of this view is presumably to be found in the half-scientific analysis of the process of sense-perception attributed to Protagoras and a variety of other thinkers in the *Theaetetus*. All things sensible, we are there told, are in a state of flux, being the product of intercourse between a constantly changing reality and a constantly changing sense-organ. Hence

Nothing is *one* thing just by itself, nor can you rightly call it by some definite name, nor even say that it is of any definite sort. On the contrary, if you call it 'large', it will be found to be also small; if 'heavy', to be also light; and so on all through, because nothing is *one* thing or *some* thing or of any definite sort. All the things we are pleased to say 'are', really are in process of becoming, as a result of movement and change and of blending one with another.[1]

Why we need to suppose that a sense-organ and that with which it has intercourse are in a state of constant change is not indicated in this passage, which accordingly seems to presuppose the point at issue. But even if this is correct, and even if, as his critics have alleged, Plato's attempts to demonstrate in individual cases that sense-particulars have contradictory attributes (e.g. that Socrates is short and tall at the same time because he is short compared with Simmias but tall compared with Cebes) are vitiated by a failure to distinguish simple from relational properties, he would still have one

1. *Theaet.*, 152D, translated by F. M. Cornford.

further argument with which to support his general position. For he could say, for example of any particular beautiful thing, that however beautiful it might appear to be its beauty could not challenge comparison with that of 'the beautiful itself', the very type and model of beauty. The latter was by definition complete and perfect in beauty; nothing else *could* be beautiful in the same way, and hence nothing else could be truly beautiful.

It is not my purpose now to estimate the force of this argument, but rather to mention some of the conclusions Plato draws from it. One such conclusion is that objects of knowledge are real, whilst those of belief are relatively unreal. To say that objects of knowledge are real is to say that they have the qualities they seem to have; they are what they appear to be. To describe the objects of belief as relatively unreal is to stress their shifting and unstable character, their tendency to manifest contradictory qualities in the way described above. A man in a state of belief, in Plato's sense of the term, is like a man in a dream: he can never fully grasp what confronts him, for it is in truth itself indefinite. The real is what we apprehend in waking consciousness; what we take to exist in dreams has at best a shadowy reality. Contrary to what is sometimes asserted, there is nothing extravagant in Plato's conception of reality; the extravagance comes, if at all, in his application of the concept. It is true that if, following G. E. Moore, we identify 'real' with 'existent' and 'unreal' with 'non-existent', we get Plato to say that objects of belief are relatively non-existent; but this is not so much a proof of Platonic absurdity as of mistaken interpretation. As Mr N. R. Murphy has argued,[1] Plato never meant to say that the things the common man supposed to exist did not exist; his point was rather that they were not what they seemed to be.

Plato does, however, carry matters to extremes in making not merely stability but absolute stability, i.e. complete freedom from change, a condition of a thing's being described as real. Objects of knowledge, according to his account, not only are what they seem to be, but further are eternally what they are. Each of them is all it is capable of being, timelessly itself. Objects of belief, as the passage quoted above makes clear, contrast with them just by failing to possess this quality; the fact that they are liable to change makes

1. In his book *The Interpretation of Plato's Republic* (Oxford, 1951).

Plato say that strictly speaking they *are* not anything at all but are merely *becoming* something. Change to Plato means variability, and variability means deceptiveness, in things just as much as in men. True reality is single and simple, appearances many and various.

Along with the contrast between knowledge and belief there thus goes another, between the realm of things that are and the realm of things which are in a state of becoming. It is Plato's thesis, as we saw at the beginning, that ordinary men, and even men with some claims to intellectual sophistication, fail entirely to recognize the existence of the first of these spheres. They are content to pass their lives on the level of particularity, i.e. to accept appearances as being authentic each as it comes. Plato's objection to this procedure is that it precludes them from ever giving an account of why things appear as they do. Their condition is, indeed, far worse than this suggests, since they are not only ignorant of true principles but quite unaware of the extent to which they are themselves deceived. Like the prisoners in the allegory of the Cave, they mistake shadows for reality and are entirely unconscious of so doing.

Odd as it may seem to modern readers who are used to quite a different conception of the subject, Plato conceives philosophy as primarily an instrument of liberation. The first task of the philosopher is to convince people of the state of ignorance in which they live, to show them that the knowledge they claim is not knowledge at all. The challenge to complacency and exposure of folly which are involved in the carrying out of this programme mean that the philosopher will be anything but popular with his fellow citizens. But Plato is quite unmoved by this prospect. For him, a philosopher is no idle commentator but a man with a mission, the mission to bring enlightenment and enable men to live as they should. The Platonic philosopher is in fact something of a prophet or a preacher, who both proclaims the truth about things and trains others, if they are willing and show sufficient aptitude, to see the truth for themselves.

A philosophical education, for Plato, has two quite distinct sides to it. It involves in the first place a rigorous intellectual training. In the seventh book of the *Republic* Plato mentions certain experiences reflection on which may initiate the progress towards philosophical truth; he also outlines a course of studies, beginning with a philosophical version of arithmetic and culminating in the synoptic study of dialectic, through which potential philosopher-kings have to pass. The emphasis throughout is on turning away from the senses and cultivating the intellect; at the highest stage of all the pupil is supposed to move entirely in a world of intelligible objects. But it would be quite wrong to take this intellectual training in isolation from its moral and emotional counterpart. Philosophy for Plato is not just an intellectual activity, even though no one can be a philosopher without undergoing elaborate intellectual exercises; it involves further a disciplining of the emotions and control of the bodily appetites. To be a philosopher, in the Platonic understanding of the term, is not merely to think but to lead a life involving a negative attitude towards sensual satisfaction. The philosopher is a man who has been able to rise superior to his passions and become, so far as a human being can, pure soul. And Plato is insistent that the connection between leading a pure life and engaging in pure thought is more than contingent. He would have found the suggestion that excellence in philosophy might coexist with moral depravity extremely repugnant.

In the *Phaedo*,[1] which purports to report Socrates' conversation on the day of his death, the philosophic life is explained as consisting in 'practising for dying'. The philosopher knows that his soul, as opposed to his body, is the element in him which has most affinity with the Forms, the true objects of knowledge. He knows further (and Socrates professes to offer proofs of the point) that his soul existed before his present bodily life and will survive his present bodily death. Given this situation, it is only logical that he should cultivate his soul and neglect his body. By refusing to gratify his bodily appetites, or rather by satisfying them to the minimum degree necessary for the continuation of life, he will keep his soul pure, and thus put it in a position to gain maximum profit when it escapes from its bodily prison and is restored to its native element. Most men fear death, but the Platonic philosopher looks forward to it, since he knows that it means not annihilation but a fuller and richer life for the most real part of himself.

Plato's belief in the immortality of the soul is seldom treated by modern philosophers with the respect accorded to his acceptance of the theory of Forms. The common tendency is to think of the

1. 63c–69e.

latter as the product of a genuine, if mistaken, piece of philosophical thinking, but to dismiss the former as little more than imaginative mythology. The fact that Plato lays so much stress on the seemingly crude notion of Recollection in his discussions of the soul's immortality encourages this conclusion. Yet there is every indication that Plato himself took the two doctrines with equal seriousness, and indeed saw a close connection between them. The dualism of intelligible reality and sense-appearances springs from the sharp contrast between the intellect and the senses, which in turn reflects a distinction of principle between the soul and the body. It would be hard to see how anyone could hold the theory of Forms without at least believing that soul and body are separable, i.e. that they are, in later philosophical language, separate in substance. If this is not enough to establish the soul's immortality, it nevertheless, as Descartes was to argue, prepares the way for that doctrine and might be said to constitute some evidence in its favour. Plato was perhaps less careful over this point than he should have been, but this is not in itself a reason for ignoring an important section of his thought.

Similarly modern Platonic scholars have little to say of the practical consequences Plato drew from his metaphysical and epistemological analyses, doubtless because they find these consequences uncongenial. Yet it would clearly be the height of absurdity to suppose that Plato was not in earnest when he made his practical recommendations. Whatever the case with some later philosophers, for him questions about the nature of things and the good life for man were closely bound up, so much so that any answer to the first must necessarily carry with it an answer to the second. That the world could be shown to be different from what it at first sight appeared to be meant that men's conduct must be different from what at first sight seemed obvious and sensible: instead of pursuing bodily pleasure they should cultivate their souls. It is important to stress this point, since some modern writers about metaphysics have argued that metaphysicians deny what everyone else takes to be obviously true but continue to act as if they did not believe their own denials: they say, for instance, that time is not real but make and keep appointments like the rest of us. Plato's case shows that this contention has less general application than may at first sight appear.[1]

1. See further Chapter 12, § 2.

2. *The nature of Forms*

Having tried to make clear that Plato is not a mere theorist, I should like now to turn back to his theory and consider some particular aspects of it. A crucial question concerns the status and function of the entities he calls Forms. Why did Plato say that there are Forms, and what problems did he suppose that the postulation of Forms solved? One line of argument to which Platonists appealed in defence of their theory of Forms was known in antiquity as 'the argument from the sciences'. It ran roughly as follows: Knowledge is possible, as the existence of geometry and arithmetic shows. Knowledge cannot be had unless there are stable entities to be known. The things we know through the senses do not fulfil this requirement, for reasons already outlined, and we must in consequence recognize the existence of entities of a different sort, inaccessible to the senses but open to the intellect, which are the true objects of scientific knowledge. It will be obvious that, as thus stated, this argument merely makes explicit the Platonic concept of knowledge and declares that it has instances; it can, however, be more plausibly restated as an argument from meaning. It will then take the form of stating that we know the meaning of certain terms such as 'straight' and 'equal', or again 'just' and 'beautiful', and cannot have learnt them in experience for the reason that nothing we meet with there truly exemplifies them. To account for our ability to use the terms meaningfully we must accordingly postulate acquaintance with 'the equal itself', 'the straight itself', etc., that is with Forms. There must be Forms, or we could not speak as we do.

Forms in this account act as patterns or standard specimens; the function of the Form of equality, for someone who wants to know whether a given pair of things are equal in some respect, is similar to that of the standard metre for someone who wants to know if a piece of material is a metre long: it can be referred to for a final decision. But this comparison is perhaps unduly flattering for Plato. The standard metre is a concrete material thing, something palpable and plain for all to see, and there is nothing mysterious about the process of consulting it. To get 'the eye of the soul', to use Plato's own expression, fixed on a Form is something altogether different, if only because Forms are explicitly said to be inaccessible to the senses. Plato nowhere gives the beginnings of an adequate account of what it is to contemplate a Form; he leaves us entirely in the dark about the shape in which such an entity is supposed to present itself to our attention. The problem may not seem acute (though in fact it is) when we consider an idea as abstract as that of equality, but it cries out for an answer when we pass to some of Plato's other examples, particularly that of the Form of bed which he uses in *Republic*, X. A craftsman, he there implies, must have the Form of bed in mind when he makes a particular bed. Does this mean that he 'sees' something in his mind's eye, and if so must not that something have definite qualities, be for example a bed of a certain size and shape? Plato makes no attempt to answer such questions either in this context or in any other, and the best we can say for him is that he probably thought of a Form as we think of a blueprint, which in a way explains the particulars made according to it without itself being another particular of the same kind. But a blueprint, though somewhat different from a unique object like the standard metre, is also something we can all get our hands on. And in any case Plato might well have said that a Form was not so much a blueprint as what made a blueprint possible.

We must leave these difficulties, and pass to another aspect of the theory. In so far as he conceived of Forms as standards, it seems that Plato thought of them as lying beyond the familiar world. The relationship of the many particulars to the one Form was said to be that of copies to an original: particulars were what they were because they each resembled the corresponding Form. There is a striking expression of this view in a passage in the *Timaeus* where the Demiurge is depicted as having created the everyday world *on the model of* the Forms; the implication is that Forms exist eternally, without regard to what goes on in the temporal sphere. All this suggests that the 'intelligible region' of Forms, as Plato himself describes it, is, in later metaphysical language, utterly transcendent of everyday experience. To pass from the state of belief to that of knowledge is, to put it crudely, to move to another and better world. But though there is much in Plato which supports this interpretation, there are also indications of another view.

In discussing the relationship of 'the one' and 'the many' Plato says sometimes that the many 'participate in' the one. This, like the explanation in terms of imitation just mentioned, is of course no more than a metaphor, but in so far as it can be taken seriously it certainly suggests a different conception of a Form from that considered above. Instead of being thought of as a standard or model a Form now becomes a structural element, and the appeal to Forms is made in the interests of explaining what occurs rather than to account for our having certain concepts.

The argument begins, as before, by stressing the fragmentary and contradictory nature of immediate experience, and by insisting that we be able to 'give an account' of phenomena. Plato dismisses the possibility that particularly careful attention to what is going on will go any way towards producing the required result: to think that these problems can be solved by using one's eyes and ears, as some contemporary students of astronomy and harmonics supposed, was to him the height of folly. The inadequacies of empiricism, the attitude of mind which sticks to the immediate facts and thinks their secret can be found by careful reflection on them, are harshly exposed in the Cave passage in *Republic*, VII. There we are told that some of the prisoners become in the course of time skilled in predicting what shadows will follow what, thanks to their having noted regularities in past experience; in the Cave itself these individuals appear to have superior wisdom. Plato, however, clearly means to suggest as he develops his allegory that they are no better off than their fellow prisoners: they have no conception of how far they are from true knowledge, and their familiarity with regular sequences in the appearances they observe in no sense amounts to understanding. The truth about things is wholly different from what anyone in the Cave supposes it to be. It seems clear enough that, in this passage and still more in the discussions of astronomy and harmonics mentioned above, Plato is insisting on the need for what would now be called a theoretical explanation of physical events; an explanation, that is to say, which exhibits these events as deducible, with a greater or less degree of accuracy, from the operation of a number of ultimate but not immediately apprehensible elements. The Forms are introduced as being just such elements. To understand what is going on in the world around us we accordingly need to rise to the apprehension of Forms.

The part played by Forms on this account of the matter is similar to that played by electrons in modern physical theory: each is postulated with the object of, in Plato's phrase, 'saving the appearances', i.e. showing why they appear as they do. Not of course that the parallel is an exact one. For one thing, the unobservables of the modern physicist are strictly unobservable: there can be no question of 'rising to the apprehension' of these fundamental particles, which was exactly what the Platonic philosophers were supposed to have done with Forms. Nor again could it be said that Plato ever suggested any mechanism by which Forms might be supposed to 'operate' as fundamental elements; the indications are, indeed, that he was unsympathetic to any form of mechanical explanation. Like many Greeks, he supposed that a proper understanding of natural processes would have to be framed in teleological terms: ideally, we should like to know why things happened, in the sense of what purpose each of them served. And though he recognized in the *Phaedo*[1] that this demand was impossible to meet, the alternative he proposed to it was not mechanical. What we should say, he tells us in that work, is that it is the presence in him of the Form of tallness which makes a man tall, not, for example, taking exercise or following some physical regimen. So far as sense can be made of this at all, it looks as if Plato is here proffering what Aristotle was later to call a formal cause explanation, as is done when someone explains a man's action by saying he was always an irascible man. A tendency of this kind is more like a force than a fundamental particle. But despite these difficulties, the parallel is sufficiently close to be instructive. Nor, of course, is it the case that theoretical explanations are confined nowadays to the physical sciences; they are to be found in the social sciences too, most prominently in economics. In so far as Plato's theory can be construed on these lines, it could certainly not be denied a strong modern interest.

Metaphysicians are often accused of being enamoured of the Beyond for its own sake: they are said to find consolation for the harsh exigencies of the common world by postulating another more agreeable realm which they insist is the only true reality. There are obvious aspects of the thought of Plato, in particular the line of argument which leads him to think of Forms as eternal patterns,

1. 95e–102a.

utterly remote from the things of sense, which suggest to the unsympathetic that he was such a metaphysician. It must be insisted, however, that the argument just expounded lends little colour to this interpretation. No one thinks of a modern physicist as enamoured of the Beyond because he postulates unobservables, which are in one sense accessible to thought alone; his purpose in doing this is plainly enough to explain what is happening here and now. Mystery-mongering and love of the occult for its own sake are the last things we associate with these procedures. Nor do we suppose that economic theorists must be escapists because the things they deal with, acts of economic men or systems of perfect competition, have no precise counterparts in the familiar world but exist only in thought: we know that their point in studying these 'ideal' entities (the phrase itself is Platonic) is to illuminate actual economic transactions. Belief in unobservables, or in objects which can be grasped by thought alone, can, as these examples show, be entirely respectable. And there is at least some ground for interpreting Plato's belief in Forms along lines like these.

It remains true, none the less, that there are quite other sides to Plato's thought. If some of his work seems to constitute a highly intelligent anticipation of modern scientific method we are not therefore entitled to conclude that his outlook is scientific through and through. He seems, for example, to have been almost totally without interest in applied science, a fact which probably goes a long way to explain his hostility to empiricism, with its stress on ability to predict and manipulate rather than understand. Nor are the implications of his concept of knowledge such as to commend themselves to cautious persons today. The central feature of his view, as I tried to bring out at the beginning, is that knowledge is a kind of vision, a seeing not with the bodily eyes but with the eye of the soul; the Forms are the object of such a knowing, and are for that reason declared to be accessible to thought alone. The gulf between this position and that which many physicists would take up about their unobservables, according to which the latter are not actual existents but theoretical constructs, is wider than at first appears: the ambiguous phrase 'accessible to thought alone' applies on both accounts, but in quite different ways. Theoretical constructs are accessible to thought alone because they exist nowhere but in thought; they are not 'objects' in the true sense at all, though they can of course be thought *about*. But Plato's Forms are accessible to thought alone because they are the objects of thought considered as a faculty of intuition, in fact as a superior sort of sensing; to treat them as mere concepts, as some modern writers have tried to do, is utterly inconsistent with Plato's general standpoint. As in the case of belief, exercise of capacity and existence of a corresponding object are necessarily bound up together: if knowing occurs at all, Forms are proved to exist. Whatever we may think of these views of Plato's, it is impossible to make any sense of his position unless we recognize that they were the views he took.

Nor is this all. Plato's equation of knowledge proper with vision leads him to stress the personal character of knowing in a way which immediately strikes the modern reader as strange. Speaking apparently of the Good, the highest and most important of the Forms, he says in a letter:

> I certainly have composed no work in regard to it, nor shall I ever do so in future; for there is no way of putting it in words like other studies. Acquaintance with it must come rather after a long period of attendance on instruction in the subject itself and of close companionship, when, suddenly, like a blaze kindled by a leaping spark, it is generated in the soul and at once becomes self-sustaining.[1]

The plain implication of this passage is that there is no such thing as Platonic philosophical doctrine, in the sense of a corpus of items of knowledge which can be immediately assented to by anyone who turns his attention to the subject. The attainment of philosophical truth is a matter of insight, an insight which supervenes on intensive intellectual effort carried out in a circle of like-minded people; the results of these operations cannot be divorced from the process of engaging in them. The contrast between this position and that taken up by many later philosophers, to say nothing of modern scientists, could scarcely be more marked. If only for this reason, Plato's philosophy, as compared with that of more orthodox writers like Descartes or Kant, has an elusive quality which makes it hard to

1. *Ep.* vii, 341c–d; translated L. A. Post.

grasp or assess. It is this feature which makes hostile critics use words like 'esoteric' and 'mystical' when they come to characterize Plato's thought. But whether Plato is as peculiar among metaphysicians as this suggests is a question which remains to be decided.

3

Metaphysics as News from Nowhere

1. *The example and the influence of Plato*

HAVING given an account of some of Plato's most prominent metaphysical views, I now want to say something of the conception of metaphysics they appear to involve. To raise the question what Plato thought about metaphysics admittedly has an artificial air, partly because he obviously had no notion of metaphysics as opposed to philosophy generally (it was not merely the word he lacked, but also the idea), partly because of the considerations just mentioned about the unsystematic character of his thought. If there was, strictly speaking, no such thing as a Platonic system, we cannot ask what sort of a thing it purported to be. But despite these difficulties the fact remains that Plato exercised an enormous influence on subsequent metaphysicians: the things he said and the things he assumed were of vital importance in determining later developments in the whole field. It is therefore useful and even necessary to proceed anachronistically and try to make his ideas about metaphysics explicit.

Let us begin by agreeing that, even had he possessed a clear concept of metaphysics, Plato would probably have made no significant distinction between philosophy and metaphysics, except perhaps to restrict the latter to theoretical scrutiny of the nature of things. If this is correct, what we need to bring out is the claims Plato made on behalf of philosophy. I suggest that these can be summarized in the following propositions, most of which will be familiar from the material discussed above.

1. The philosopher has knowledge as opposed to opinion or

belief: his thought is clear and connected where the thought of other men is confused and fragmentary.

2. The philosopher has access to real things which are stable, unchanging and for that reason fully knowable; he therefore recognizes sense-appearances for what they are, inconstant, flickering, unreal like dream-objects.

3. The philosopher will not accept appearances at their face value; it is his aim to penetrate behind appearances and to explain them in the light of first principles.

4. Philosophy differs from other branches of enquiry (e.g. geometry) (a) in taking nothing for granted; (b) in its scope, which is universal; (c) in being fully intellectual, in no way dependent on sense-experience.

5. Philosophy aims at changing men's lives by revealing the truth about things, which is very different from what is commonly thought.

Before proceeding it may be useful to elaborate the fourth of these propositions. The first point to make clear is that, in discussing the contrast between philosophy and other branches of enquiry, Plato is limiting the scope of the latter severely. Activities like medicine or engineering were not recognized by him as embodying genuine knowledge; he was inclined to think of them rather as mere know-how, successful perhaps in practice but quite unsupported by theory. The only sciences he thought worth consideration in this context were mathematics, astronomy and harmonics. Nor was his opinion even of these studies one of unqualified admiration. In a remarkable passage in the *Republic*[1] he accused mathematicians of passing their lives in a dream-state, on the ground that they started with assumptions which they made no attempt to justify and proceeded complacently to grant each other conclusions for which they had insufficient warrant—not, apparently, because their arguments were lacking in rigour but because the premises were inadequately supported. In contrasting 'dialectic' with studies like these Plato is at pains to suggest that the dialectician or philosopher is as much concerned with starting-points as with what follows from them; it is his aim to eliminate the hypothetical element in knowledge by

1. 533b–c.

justifying initial assumptions in the light of an unhypothetical first principle. What precisely the carrying out of this programme would involve is far from clear, but its elaboration is at least intended to suggest that philosophy is fully self-critical, as opposed to the other sciences whose exponents are blinkered.

The universal character of philosophy is connected with the same point. According to Plato, arithmetic assumes the notions of odd and even number, geometry that of three kinds of angle, and neither makes any attempt to justify or examine its assumption. But philosophy's first concern is with assumptions, as we have seen, and in attempting to remove their hypothetical character (i.e. to convert them from assumptions into demonstrated truths) it necessarily widens the scope of the sciences to which they belong. The barriers between separate studies disappear as they are each seen as falling within a larger enquiry, and the logical end of the process, indicated rather than explained by Plato, is that they should all merge into one, the supreme synoptic study of dialectic. We should like to know much more about Plato's conception of dialectic, but at least we know that it was intended to be universal in its scope. Similarly we know that it was supposed to be purely intellectual in its method, to 'begin with Forms, proceed through Forms and end in Forms', as Plato puts it in one passage.[1] It was one of Plato's complaints against mathematics that mathematicians were too dependent on sensible helps; it was of the essence of geometrical argument, for example, that the geometrician should draw or imagine figures. Philosophical thinking was to be free of this defect too; it was to be completely rigorous, a matter of the pure intellect, the intellect uncontaminated by sense.

The details of these contentions matter less for our present purposes than their general drift: the point that deserves emphasis is the way in which the claims made by Plato recur over and over again in the history of metaphysics. Refusal to accept the deliverances of the senses at their face value, on the ground that they are mutually contradictory; the argument that we must go behind these 'appearances' to a deeper 'reality' which will alone explain why they take the form they do; the contention that pure thought will put us in touch with this deeper reality: these are continuing themes in this

1. *Republic*, 511c.

branch of thought. So is the contention that over and above the various departmental branches of learning there must be a single synoptic science, concerned, as Aristotle put it, with 'reality as such' or with the 'most real' of all things.

Admittedly the form in which these conclusions were urged, and the arguments used to support them, varied widely from time to time. To mention only the most obvious sort of difference, those philosophers who worked inside the general framework of Christianity were apt, in contrast to Plato, to put God at the centre of their account of reality: arguments for the existence of Forms were replaced by arguments for God's existence. Developments in areas of thought outside philosophy affected, if not the way in which different philosophers saw their fundamental task, at least some details of the solutions they put forward. Thus the metaphysics of Aquinas, which were framed at a time when the rediscovered ideas of Aristotle had to be squared with Christian theology, were significantly different from those of Descartes, who found it necessary to allow more weight than any of his predecessors to the truth embodied in the mechanical view of the world favoured by the rising physical sciences of his time, or again from those of Kant, who was troubled by the advance of the social sciences and the threat this seemed to constitute to morality. The notion that all major European philosophers have produced scarcely distinct versions of a single *philosophia perennis* would be absurd even if we were willing to agree that metaphysicians were the only philosophers. Yet it is possible to see among the great metaphysical writers both a common conception of what had to be done and a certain area of agreement about how to do it. That this should be so is without doubt due to the influence of the ideas and example of Plato.

We can, indeed, go further than this. In the Introduction to this book we mentioned some of the charges brought against metaphysics by critically minded philosophers in the course of the last two hundred years. Metaphysics, we have been told over and over again, is not a serious discipline but a pseudo-science; the propositions of which it purports to consist are such that no means exist for determining whether they are true or false. The pronouncements of metaphysicians must in these circumstances be set down as entirely lacking in real significance, and the adjective 'metaphysical' henceforth figure exclusively as a term of abuse. Now while it would not be correct to connect this attitude of suspicion of and hostility towards metaphysics with exclusive antipathy to Plato, it is certainly true that a particular conception of the thought of Plato, and of the claims Plato made on behalf of philosophy, has affected discussion of the whole subject. What may be called the standard conception of metaphysics as seen by these anti-metaphysical writers is widely supposed to have originated in Plato.

Let me, at the cost of possible repetition, make this conception explicit. The view is that metaphysics is the science of things unseen. It is superior to other disciplines in several ways: because of the greater reality of its objects, which are stable where the objects of everyday experience are unstable; because of its comprehensive character; because of the absolute certainty of its pronouncements. Its propositions derive their certainty from the fact that they owe nothing to the deliverances of the senses but have each been proved at the bar of reason. And they serve to express fundamental truths, because things unseen underlie things seen, which are nothing but their appearances.

2. Kant's criticism of metaphysics

This is the conception of metaphysics assumed by Kant and dismissed as impossible in the *Critique of Pure Reason*, the most thorough and devastating of all anti-metaphysical writings. It is true that Kant derived his ideas about metaphysics not directly from Plato, but rather from the inferior successors of Leibniz on whose textbooks he was required to lecture. If we look at his detailed exposure of metaphysical arguments we see that it is arranged with Alexander Baumgarten's *Metaphysica* in mind: Kant deals with 'rational psychology', 'rational cosmology' and 'natural theology' just as Baumgarten does, and prefaces this part of his work, again like Baumgarten, with an elaborate treatment of the claims of 'ontology', the alleged study of 'being as such'. But though these local influences are strong (they affect in particular the question of the logical status of metaphysical propositions, a question whose importance was scarcely recognized before Descartes), it would be false to suppose that Kant was exclusively subject to them. There is, on the contrary, strong evidence, both in the *Critique* itself and in its forerunner the inaugural *Dissertation* of 1770, that he felt it necessary to come to terms with Platonism. Kant was convinced that Plato was right to recognize the existence of a world of unseen or intelligible entities lying behind the appearances of sense; without that assumption morality would not make sense. But he was also sure that Plato and those who followed him were misled in believing that we could have knowledge of this supersensible reality. There was, in truth, no knowledge except through sense-experience, with the result that the whole metaphysical enterprise turned out to be an impossible one.

I shall not enquire at this point whether Kant was correct in his characterization of metaphysics as supposed knowledge of the supersensible; it is sufficient that this was both a plausible view and one widely accepted both in Kant's time and since. Nor, of course, is this the place to discuss the consistency of Kant's own position, which is obviously open to question. The grounds on which Kant rejected the possibility of metaphysical knowledge can be examined without special reference to either point.

Kant may be said to have had both empirical and *a priori* arguments against the possibility of metaphysics. His empirical argument was based on the actual fact of metaphysical disagreement: he simply pointed to the undeniable circumstance that metaphysicians had argued about many issues for a long time without showing the slightest sign of settling anything. Thus attempts had been made for hundreds of years to produce definitive arguments for God's existence or a knockdown proof of the freedom of the will, but the advocates of atheism and determinism had not been silenced: there seemed, indeed, to be as good a case on the one side as the other. A science in which this sort of thing could happen was to say the least a curious one.

But Kant did not rest his case exclusively, or even mainly, on these *ad hominem* considerations. He directed his attention, with a sure instinct for the crucial point, to the nature of human knowledge, and cut the ground from beneath Platonism by demonstrating that the human intellect is in no sense a faculty of intuition. Men could form the notion of an intuitive understanding, but they had

only to do so to see that their own reason was not, as such an understanding would be, a primary source of knowledge, but a discursive
instrument parasitic upon the senses. The possibility of an intellectual vision of ultimate reality, such as Plato had canvassed, could
thus be firmly discounted. Nor for that matter was it possible to
defend a weaker version of Platonism, according to which truth
about the intelligible world could be come by through a series of
arguments which took their start from what is experienced. Kant
admitted the plausibility of this suggestion, whose strength lay, he
believed, in our undoubted possession of a special set of concepts
he called categories. But though he never ceased to emphasize the
non-empirical nature of these concepts, he was clear that their
proper function was not to lead us outside the empirical sphere but
to provide a framework inside which empirical questions could be
asked. Contrary to what he had once thought himself, these 'pure
intellectual concepts', whose very description has a strongly Platonic
ring, were not available for use in metaphysics, or at least not in
metaphysics of the Platonic type. Involved in the meaning of each
one of them there was a reference to time, when the 'reality' they were
supposed to apply to was by definition timeless. To try to apply a
concept of this kind outside the range of possible experience, as was
done for instance in the First Cause argument for God's existence,
was accordingly to say nothing definite. Remove the reference to
time involved in the notion of cause (the element on which Hume
had laid such stress) and nothing intelligible remains.

Kant reinforced these arguments when he asked his celebrated
question, 'How are synthetic *a priori* judgments possible?'. Here
again his eye for a point of central importance was unerring. The
propositions of metaphysics, according to the account we have
examined above, claim to be completely certain; there can be no
question of our being wrong about them, as we clearly can be wrong
in our sense-judgments. This means that they are one and all necessary truths, to use a terminology Kant inherited from his predecessors,
or *a priori* truths, in his own barbarous variation on this terminology.
But as well as being necessary they also claim to be informative:
they purport to say how things are, not merely to make explicit what
is contained in the concepts of which they consist.

Now the question can be raised: suppose that the propositions of metaphysics really did answer this description, how could we know them to be true? Kant tackles this question by generalizing it: he asks in what circumstances we can formulate judgments which are synthetic (non-tautologous) and necessary of any kind. His own view was that there were at least two fields in which human beings do make such judgments, namely in mathematics and in what he called 'pure physics'; 'The internal angles of a Euclidean triangle add up to two right angles' and 'Every change has a cause' were, for him, both synthetic *a priori* truths. But the results of his elaborate examination of the circumstances in which we arrive at truths of this sort was far from encouraging for supporters of metaphysics. That synthetic *a priori* judgments were possible in the two spheres named was not to be ascribed to the possession by the human mind of a power of insight into the structure of fact, for neither sort of statement was a statement of fact in the full sense of the term. Pure mathematics Kant connected, in a way few later philosophers have found convincing, with space and time, which he thought to be formal conditions of human perception; to elicit what was spatially and temporally possible, as in fact mathematicians did on this view of the matter, was to elicit conditions of fact. Similarly pure physics was occupied not with what actually was the case but with the presuppositions of an enquiry into what is the case; its judgments were not factual but rather had the force of prescriptions. They were principles used in the exploration of experience, empty and abstract until brought to bear on empirical data. And as such they could give little comfort to the metaphysician, either as affording instances of purely rational knowledge or as constitutive principles in his own science.

There are, naturally, many points in these analyses to which later critics have taken exception. Kant's philosophy of mathematics is particularly hard to defend, though there are still philosophers who maintain on different grounds that the propositions of pure mathematics are both necessary and synthetic. Nor, of course, has Kant's attempt to show that there are and must be synthetic *a priori* principles conditioning experience, as he takes the causal principle and the principle of substance to do, won universal favour. But the question of the tenability of his positive doctrines here can be separated from that of the correctness of his criticism of metaphysics.

Even those who are most sceptical of the possibility of there being any valid synthetic *a priori* judgments tend to think that Kant was entirely correct in holding that metaphysical propositions would, if genuine, answer to this description. They praise him for asking the question how metaphysics could be possible, and agree that its possibility would involve a claim to rational insight into the structure of fact, a claim which can certainly not be supported by reference to the sort of cases Kant examines. Whatever the value of his discussions of these cases (and I should like to make clear that I do not share the critics' attitude over pure physics at least), there can be no doubt whatever that his discussion of the nature of metaphysical statements goes right to the heart of the matter.

The position Kant himself takes up is that metaphysical pronouncements purport to be synthetic but are in fact analytic. They are, that is to say, verbal rather than real. Every system of metaphysics consists first in the positing of certain definitions and second in deducing the logical consequences of these definitions. The necessity which seemingly attaches to metaphysical propositions springs from the circumstance that, for anyone who accepts the initial definitions, there really is no denying them, since they merely make explicit what the definitions involve. The whole value of a metaphysical system thus turns on the value to be attached to the definitions of its primary concepts. And it is Kant's thesis that these can at best be verbal, since the concepts in question are, unlike the categories of the understanding, incapable of being schematized. We cannot, that is to say, indicate what such concepts mean in concrete terms, as we can indicate what 'cause' means when we connect the idea with that of invariable succession, or 'substance' when we connect it with the notion of what persists through temporal change. Cause and substance as they function in metaphysical thinking are supposed to be free of these temporal encumbrances, but when we ask what is left once the reference to time is removed the answer is far from satisfactory. We are left, in fact, with purely logical ideas, which can be explained verbally but are totally inadequate for the precise characterization of specific situations. The result is that whilst the metaphysician in a way contrives to say something, he does not succeed in saying anything about anything in particular, and his whole theory therefore remains in the air.

3. *Criticisms of metaphysics: the Positivists and Kant*

Kant's criticism of metaphysics compares favourably at more points than one with the more virulent denunciations of the subject produced by Logical Positivists. For one thing, Kant himself had clearly felt the urge to move from the sensible to the supersensible, as he was inclined to put it: he knew from experience what it was like to want to construct a metaphysical system. The Positivists, by contrast, were apt to think of metaphysics as something of which its exponents should be ashamed; few of them had made a sympathetic study of even a single metaphysical writer. Seeing metaphysics from a distance, they naturally had a somewhat imperfect view of its attractions and subtleties. As is well known, they dismissed metaphysical pronouncements as 'literally senseless', on the ground that they could not be brought to the test of experience; to bring this conclusion home their practice was to select individual sentences from treatises of metaphysics and ask how anyone would set about verifying or falsifying them. That such sentences might not be intelligible in isolation—that the concepts they contained might need to be related to a whole set of connected concepts to become meaningful—does not seem to have occurred to them. Nor did they show much awareness of the profound difference in logical status between the highly abstract ideas of metaphysics and simple empirical notions; they seemed to think that if a word like 'monad' had meaning, we ought to be able to point to cases to which it applied in the way in which we can point to cases to which 'chair' or 'horse' applies. Kant was altogether more sophisticated than that. He knew very well that metaphysical concepts are, by the admission of those who father them, remote from sense, and that the question of how they come to have meaning is correspondingly complicated. It is for this reason that he gives such prominence to the problem of schematism: as he says in one passage, schemata are to pure intellectual concepts what examples are to empirical concepts. To show that a pure intellectual concept can be used with full significance we must be able to point to its schema, which is in effect its spatio-temporal counterpart. Kant thinks we can do that for the categories of the understanding, which have an exclusively empirical use, but not for the concepts of metaphysics, which are accordingly without real significance.

The differences between Kant and the Positivists over metaphysics should nevertheless not be exaggerated. They agree in thinking that the essential aim of metaphysicians is to inform us about a reality supposed to lie entirely outside the range of sense-experience. They agree that if metaphysical pronouncements are to make sense, they must in some way be related to everyday experience. And they both conclude that metaphysics is unable to satisfy this test, with the result that the news it professes to purvey is really news from nowhere. The differences between them concern matters of detail, though not unimportant matters of detail. On the question of meaning in particular Kant seems to be clearly the better. He does not say, as the Positivists did, that metaphysical sentences are meaningless; he recognizes, indeed, that in one way they are perfectly meaningful, since the concepts which figure in them can certainly be explained verbally.[1] The pronouncements of metaphysicians have their own internal logic; there are right and wrong ways of taking them. But Kant rightly insisted that this is not enough to prove that they have any real significance. The possibility remains, after all, that the metaphysician's whole activity is essentially idle, a game conducted according to rules but serving no purpose outside itself. It may be, in fact, that metaphysics falls down by lacking not so much sense as reference; what it says is, in its own way, intelligible, but the difficulty is to find what is being talked about. By pointing up this possibility and demanding that metaphysicians meet it Kant presented them with a more serious challenge than any of their later critics.

Kant and the Positivists have somewhat different answers to the question what prompts otherwise intelligent men to spend their lives in what they both regard as the wasted activity of constructing or debating metaphysical systems. Kant speaks of human reason as being under a 'natural illusion', as a result of which metaphysical questions constantly occur to it. The illusion in question is that of supposing that the world of nature is independently existent; thinking of it in that way we are naturally led to think there must be something beyond it which explains why it is as it is. The hankering after the supersensible already mentioned encourages this tendency:

1. Cf. *Critique of Pure Reason*, B186/A147 in this connection.

we are all prone, for moral reasons, to believe that this is not the only world, and it is not surprising that we should want to know what the realm to which we belong as moral beings is like. Explanations of this sort had little appeal for the Positivists, whose conception of morals was quite different, though they recognized, and indeed emphasized, that there was an element of escapism about metaphysics which made it congenial to the tender-minded. So far as they took metaphysics seriously, they tended to see it as primarily the product of bad logic. Metaphysicians, they said, were led to ask impossible and unanswerable questions because, for instance, they supposed that there must be some single entity corresponding to the common noun 'man', or again because they failed to see the distinction between the force which the word 'is' has when used predicatively (as in 'Socrates is wise') and that it has when used existentially (as in 'There is no such thing as a centaur'). The first mistake had betrayed Plato into his theory of Forms, the second into his view that the world of sense is only partly real: he had moved from 'This object is both beautiful and not beautiful' to 'This object both is and is not'. It was felt to be some excuse for these blunders that the science of formal logic had remained in a primitive condition, without offering an adequate account of the variety of statements people actually make, until shortly before the Positivists' own time. Thus Bradley might not have made the mistakes he did had he known about and appreciated the logical writings of his contemporary Frege.

The odd thing about this particular suggestion is that Bradley was certainly familiar with the distinction between grammatical and logical form; that there are many more types of judgment than those recognized in traditional logic was a major theme of his own book on the subject. It would be quite wrong to think of him as logically unsophisticated. Nor is it in general true that great metaphysical philosophers have been insensitive to logical distinctions. Plato himself pointed out the difference between the predicative and existential use of 'is' in his discussion of negation in the *Sophist*; Aristotle's doctrine of categories is an exploration of a different, though not wholly unrelated, series of ambiguities in the use of the verb 'to be'. Leibniz' interest, and partial anticipation of future developments, in formal logic are notorious. That these celebrated writers should, despite their logical discoveries, have continued with their attempts to arrive at metaphysical truth would suggest that the Positivist account of the matter cannot be more than partially correct. It may cover particular arguments used by metaphysicians (the Ontological Proof of God's existence is on the face of things its most convincing exemplification),[1] but it cannot pretend to offer the whole story of why men are drawn to metaphysics.

The truth is, indeed, that neither the Positivists nor Kant satisfy us on this vital topic; and one explanation of this may be that their common conception of metaphysics as the supposed science of things supersensible is less authentic than they imagine. I have suggested above that this conception was based on a certain interpretation of the philosophy of Plato, and I do not wish to argue now that it was anything but a plausible interpretation. Plato's dichotomy of Being and Becoming, the first knowable by the pure intellect, the second the object of the senses, is quite naturally taken as Kant and the Positivists took it; the Platonic philosopher, as we have seen, claims intimate knowledge of a class of entities whose very existence is not suspected by the common man, and suggests that truth can be come by only if men will disregard the evidence of their bodily eyes and turn their attention to the Forms which are accessible only to the eye of the soul. To describe Plato's outlook as 'other-worldly' is in these circumstances not extravagant. Nor, of course, is Plato the only philosopher on whose thought such a construction can be naturally put. As I have pointed out, Platonic themes occur repeatedly in the course of European metaphysical thought, with the result that a conception of metaphysics which fits the case of Plato will have pretty general application.

It remains possible, even so, that to condemn them as purveyors of news from nowhere is unfair to metaphysicians, or at least to some metaphysicians. It is not even certain that it is wholly fair to Plato: if we point up the passages in which Forms are introduced with the object of 'saving the appearance' we find ourselves with a Plato whose interests are firmly in the here and now rather than in the Beyond for its own sake. So far from being hostile to science, as metaphysicians are commonly said by Positivists to be, the Plato of these passages seems to have an extraordinarily clear grasp of the

1. Though cf. p. 128 below.

principles of scientific method. I have given reasons already for thinking that it is misleading to take such passages in isolation, but the very fact that they occur shows that Plato's case is a good deal more complicated than some of his less friendly readers have supposed. And even if it were not—even if it answered exactly to the model of metaphysics set up by the critics we have examined—we could not conclude with confidence that all metaphysical thought conforms to the same pattern. The influence of Plato has been very large, but it has sometimes been exercised in a negative way: people have seen the example of Plato as something to be avoided rather than imitated. It is not surprising that philosophers have put forward metaphysical theories which are, on the face of it, very different from the Platonic type of theory: this-worldly rather than other-worldly, concerned to tell us how to take what falls within experience rather than urge us to abandon the familiar world for contemplation of a better world which lies beyond the reach of the senses. The impetus to construct metaphysical theories of this kind is clearly different from that considered above, as is the logical character of the propositions of which they consist; arguments which are valid against the possibility of metaphysics as Plato is held to have conceived it may well not be destructive of metaphysics in this form. In fact, the recognition of this second kind of metaphysical theory opens afresh the whole question of the nature and validation of metaphysical statements.

But before pursuing these matters further it will be well to consider some examples.

4

Materialism and Aristotelianism

1. *The philosophy of materialism*

WHEN people discuss metaphysical questions today, in the course of real life as opposed to that of academic study, they commonly find themselves arguing for or against materialism. It is one of the oddities of European thought that the philosophy of materialism has nowhere found adequate expression, Thomas Hobbes being the only philosopher of the first rank to have shown any sympathy with it. But it has appealed to a large number of secondary thinkers, from Democritus and Epicurus in the ancient world onwards; its claims were canvassed with enthusiasm at the time of the Enlightenment, treated with seriousness by Hegel and debated with passion throughout the nineteenth century. More recently it has been prominent in American thought, under the slightly disguised name of 'naturalism'. It also has, of course, the dubious distinction of forming part of the official corpus of communist beliefs.

What exactly is materialism, and what sorts of issue does it raise? In answering these questions the first requisite is to set aside as irrelevant the usage of the term 'materialist' to denote a person who prefers sensual pleasures over states which are commonly thought to be more estimable. Materialism of this moral sort, the favourite target of preachers and newspaper editors, may or may not be held along with metaphysical materialism, but the two have nothing essentially to do with one another. It is certainly not immoral to accept materialism as a system of speculative ideas, whatever objections there may be to it on other grounds.

One obvious way of taking materialism is as a doctrine of what there is, an account of the ultimate nature of things. The central proposition of the materialist, on this view, is that nothing exists except matter, or rather material substance and its modifications. The qualification is necessary because there is plainly a sense in which all sorts of non-material things can be said to exist, for example thoughts and feelings, or the spirit of the age. The materialist does not deny these obvious facts, but argues that the things in question (a) are not independent existences, and (b) can be adequately explained as modifications of matter, without the need to postulate spirits or spiritual substances.

The first of these points is a good deal easier than the second. It can be made intelligible by the consideration that there could be no such thing as thoughts or feelings unless someone or something thought or felt, just as there could be no such thing as the spirit of the age unless there were persons, institutions or ways of proceeding to embody it. A thought existing without relation to a thinker is either an abstraction or an impossibility. To think of it as independently real is like thinking of a quality as existing independently of the thing it qualifies; it is like thinking that you could have the grin of the Cheshire cat without the cat. In one sense of course you could, since you could abstract it and consider it in isolation, but in another sense you could not: for the grin to be there the cat would have to be there too.

The presupposition of this analysis, which was embodied in the classical metaphysical distinctions of substance, attribute and mode, is that whenever anything happens the question can be asked: what is it happening to? The idea is that there must be ultimate subjects of predication which have qualities or stand in relations; reference to these must be made if we are to understand the existence of anything else. Thus according to the classical account of the matter we cannot understand the notion of *murder* without thinking of two or more persons as standing in a certain relationship, or of *space* without thinking of material bodies as being at a certain distance and in certain directions from each other. Murder and space in these examples could be said to be abstract, persons and material bodies concrete.

Materialism and its rivals come into the picture when those who accept the foregoing analysis proceed to enquire into the nature of what I have called above 'ultimate subjects of predication'. The adjective 'ultimate' itself is ominous, implying as it does that an answer at the level of common sense will not satisfy. Why should we not simply say that e.g. men and machines are concrete, whilst intelligence and speed are abstract? One consideration which is adduced against this view is that machines at least can be analysed further; they can readily be thought of as e.g. pieces of metal, etc. arranged in a certain way. The same sort of thing can be said of other artefacts, and even of natural objects like mountains and rocks. In each case if we ask 'What is it that is ultimately concerned here?', we tend to be driven away from the first obvious answers, and find ourselves invoking entities a good deal less palpable than sticks and stones. It is to material particles, or whatever their ultimate constituents may be, that we suppose that things happen in the physical world.

Descartes in the seventeenth century reached this sort of conclusion about things physical; he believed that natural objects, animate as well as inanimate, were all differentiations or modifications of a single underlying material substance. But he was not a materialist because, although he was prepared to think of animals as no more than highly complex machines, he would not apply the same analysis to human beings. Men had spiritual as well as physical properties; in giving an account of them we must reckon with mental as well as physical phenomena. And mental phenomena could not be seen as accidents of material substance; to understand them we must postulate a mind or soul in which or to which they happened. Thus minds or spirits or souls were among the ultimate constituents of the universe, as well as material substance.

The thesis of materialism was not unknown to Descartes: it was canvassed in his day by Hobbes and Gassendi. But it seemed to him absurd, since it flew in the face of the evident facts of consciousness. The feeling of hunger, he argued, was at once utterly different and completely separate from the 'indescribable twitching of the stomach' which regularly went with it. Thoughts and acts of will were still more obviously distinct from their physical concomitants: they could be apprehended and identified as spiritual immediately. The fact of mind was the surest of all facts: it was the one fact whose existence could not be denied without falling into self-contradiction.

These arguments of Descartes remain almost as persuasive today as they were when first formulated, yet there are ways in which a materialist could try to meet them without having to deny the obvious. One would be to follow the line taken by Professor Ryle and offer a reinterpretation of the terms in which we speak of mental phenomena. Professor Ryle is not himself a materialist, but his emphasis on bodily behaviour as not merely manifesting but being the working of mind, together with his attempt to dispense with all specifically mental happenings (acts of will or insight), can be and have been taken as supporting a materialist view. The life of the mind as Professor Ryle sees it, so far from being something separate from the life of the body, is unthinkable apart from the latter; and this applies not merely to pedestrian matters but to the highest spiritual activities. Even a Plato shows that he is thinking in his face and his movements; complete physical immobility, if compatible with mental activity at all, is attained only by the strictest self-control, i.e. by a deliberate physical effort. For most of us, most of the time, being engaged in thought means, quite simply, doing something physical.

The strength of this *behaviourist* analysis of mental-conduct words, as Ryle rather awkwardly calls them, is in the flood of light it throws on a wide range of ideas whose logical status was radically misconceived by the Cartesians. It is obvious enough, when we think of it, that to speak of a man's character or abilities is not to say anything of what is occurring in his mind at any particular time, but to refer to what he tends or is in a position to do. To describe someone as having certain beliefs, or as being knowledgeable on a particular subject, can similarly be analysed indirectly in terms of his potential actions, provided we include speaking and writing among these. Nor is the ingenious construction put by this school on alleged acts of will and insight, which figured so prominently in the Cartesian picture of the mind, open to immediate objection. Ryle, following Wittgenstein here, suggests that when a man 'grasps' a point or 'sees' the bearing of an argument the terms in quotation marks do not describe a special intellectual act, as Descartes (and for that matter Plato) supposed, but rather mark the termination of a process of puzzlement; to say I see something, in the ordinary use of the term, is to report a success, and similarly with the metaphorical use. A parallel account can be given of acts of will. When I say that it is my firm decision to do something or other I report on my intentions, which are not episodes in my mental life; and when at a particular moment I give my decision, I do not report an episode either. To say that I have now made up my mind is to signal the end of a period of uncertainty; any apparent experience of choosing which may accompany it is in fact irrelevant. I can make up my mind without having any special feeling, and I could have the feeling in question without having really made up my mind.[1]

But whatever conviction the theory carries over individual points, it seems when interpreted in the way most congenial to materialism to involve the absurdity of denying that there is such a thing as an inner mental life. It is one thing to insist that the terms in which we appraise mental qualities are unintelligible without reference to what the subjects of those qualities do, and quite another to say that we can find the whole meaning of such terms in overt actions. And even if we could, it would not follow that the thesis of materialism was proved, for an action is something undertaken by a living human being, not by a mere material body: corpses do no actions. It is for this reason, among others, that Ryle strongly repudiates the charge of being a materialist: he wants to make neither bodies nor minds but *persons* the ultimate subjects of human actions.[2] To make materialism plausible a further step has to be taken: the behaviour of persons has to be explained, and explained convincingly, in material or natural terms. Most of the current controversy about materialism turns on whether such an explanation can be given.

For the purposes of this controversy it is not important that the materialist should take up an extreme behaviourist or physicalist view on the meaning of mental-conduct terms; he can allow that there are specifically mental phenomena, provided only that he denies that they occur in or presuppose an independent mental substance. He needs, that is to say, to go along with Ryle only so far as the negative side of the case is concerned, though there is nothing to prevent him from embracing full-scale behaviourism if he can make it plausible. What is really important for him is not so much the nature of mental life as its explanation. He has to show, in

1. All these arguments are to be found in Wittgenstein's *Investigations*; compare also the index to Ryle's *Concept of Mind*, s.v. 'achievements'.
2. Cf. in this connection P. F. Strawson: *Individuals*, Chapter 3, where the point is made explicitly.

effect, that, whatever form they take, mental phenomena are what they are because of the working of factors outside themselves, factors of a material kind. And it must be admitted that there is at least some evidence which tells in favour of this view.

The kind of evidence I have in mind in making this statement is the following. First, the achievements of exponents of cybernetics in constructing machines which display mind-like behaviour, and thus suggest that human beings too may be nothing but highly complicated mechanisms. Secondly, the success of sociologists in showing the extent to which ideas, and indeed whole ways of thinking, are socially conditioned, so much so that to explain why they were held we have to look not at the reasons which those who embraced them put forward in their support, but rather at the factors in the environment which made it natural to hold them. Thirdly, the existence of theories like the Freudian theory of religion which, whatever its particular plausibility, has the general effect of suggesting that men do not really understand why they act as they do, but are actuated by forces over whose build-up and operation they are unable to exercise control. The important thing about these and similar considerations is not so much their individual as their cumulative weight. It is when they are taken together that they point to the conclusion that mental phenomena cannot be properly investigated at their own level but need to be explained from outside to become truly intelligible.

Materialism as I have just been expounding it is no longer an account of what there is but a thesis about the proper way to take things. It amounts in effect to an assertion of the omnicompetence of science. More accurately, it amounts to saying that natural scientists alone can give a *satisfactory* explanation of why things are what they are. That other types of explanation are sometimes available need not be denied by the materialist; he need not even deny them a certain validity at their own level. What he has to insist on is that their importance for the purposes of theoretical understanding is negligible when compared with that of the explanations given by scientists. If we want the last word on these matters—and it is just this that we want as metaphysicians—it is to scientists that we must turn. It is important to notice that more is involved in this position than the claim that there is no topic on which the scientist is not at liberty to pronounce if he chooses. Scientists can and do claim the right to investigate, say, the phenomena of religion or the workings of the human mind without taking up any metaphysical position; they do this so long as they are content to see their own approach to such topics as neither excluding nor being excluded by other ways of taking them. But there is, whether rightly or wrongly (I discuss this point in a later chapter), a strong pressure to move from this *neutralist* position to one in which one or other point of view is preferred over the rest. To give overall preference to the scientific point of view is to embrace the philosophy of materialism.

It may well be objected to the foregoing account that it proceeds on the assumptions (a) that it is possible to speak without serious distortion of a *single* scientific point of view, and (b) that the expressions 'to explain something in material terms' and 'to explain something in natural terms' can be equated. That it does proceed on these assumptions may be admitted, but it does not follow that the whole discussion is invalidated. For my purpose in this short sketch has obviously not been to put forward a metaphysical theory in detail, but rather to outline as much of one as is necessary for there to be an intelligent discussion of its logical character. The points involved in the assumptions would clearly have to be gone into at length if we were discussing materialism itself, but do not need prolonged consideration now. It will be sufficient if we notice that the level of generality we ascribe to the term 'materialism' will vary according to the views we take on the issues raised. Should it turn out that the theory, once virtually orthodox, that all other sciences can in principle be reduced to physics is no longer capable of defence, we shall have to acknowledge that 'materialism' will be a generic term: it will cover a number of similar doctrines instead of a single specific doctrine, and it will be in order to ask a man who professes it what version of it he follows. To make the whole position plausible would obviously in these circumstances be far from easy, since arguments which seem impressive on the assumption of the unity of science would then be less so, but it would not for that reason be impossible. Materialism is certainly a good deal easier to understand and present on the other view, which is taken by most of its supporters and assumed without discussion in most popular debates on the subject. And this being the case we may perhaps be permitted to continue with the easier version for our present limited purposes.

To recapitulate: we first defined materialism as an ontological doctrine, that is to say as an account of the nature of the ultimate subjects of predication in the world. Materialism on this view holds that there are, at bottom, no other substances than material substances, and it supports its assertion both by a polemic directed against the very possibility of mental or spiritual substance and by arguments which purport to show that non-material phenomena are in some way attributable to the workings of matter. It was in this connection that we introduced the Ryle/Wittgenstein view of the import of mental-conduct terms, which certainly seems, if pressed to extremes, to support materialism by explaining the meaning of those terms with exclusive reference to bodily actions. But apart from the difficulties of this attempted explanation, it is arguable that it would not, even if successful, justify the conclusion at which the materialist wants to arrive, since it would leave persons, as opposed to material bodies, as ultimate subjects of predication. To complete the materialist case we therefore need to turn our attention to the activities of persons, and show that these can all be understood in terms of the operation of external factors.[1] This amounts, in effect, to accepting the final validity of the scientific view of the world, which sees actions as brought about by causes outside the agent's control, instead of being freely chosen as a result of his decisions and justified by reference to grounds. The plausibility of materialism as a form of metaphysics turns on whether we think the case for this paradoxical preference has been made out.

2. The philosophy of Aristotle

It is not my intention at this stage either to discuss the merits of materialism as such or to enter into a comparison of its logical status with that of Platonism. Before embarking on any such comparison

1. Obviously there are different ways of satisfying this requirement too. Freud's metaphysical outlook was strongly naturalistic, but his psychology is by no means so obviously framed in material terms as that of, say, Hobbes on the one hand and 'drive' theorists on the other. In a full discussion of materialism it would be most important to consider just what kinds of natural explanation of human behaviour must be demanded by the materialist. But it is not necessary to go into the question now.

it will be useful to consider another example of a metaphysical system, one which turns out to bear important resemblances to both the theories so far examined. I refer to the metaphysics of Aristotle. Aristotle defines 'first philosophy', which was his term for metaphysics, in two apparently quite different ways. He says in one place, following here a line of thought which is broadly Platonic, that it is the science of 'pure form'. Pure form is exemplified by God and the intelligences which move the heavenly spheres, whose existence is supposed to be proved by arguments which begin from familiar facts (e.g. the fact of motion) but terminate in entities which can be grasped only by the intelligence. Aristotle differs from Plato in not suggesting that pure form is the only reality, but he does hold that it is the most important of all things, since everything else is causally dependent on it. To put it crudely but not inaccurately: but for the existence of God, the Unmoved Mover, nothing would be able to go round the world, and so the whole cosmos would be impossible.

The God of Aristotle is very different from the God of religious men (it would be quite absurd to think of worshipping a deity whose sole interest is in himself), but he is not so different from the God of later philosophical theology or the Absolute of more secular thinkers. He resembles the last two in being conceived as a First Cause or Ultimate Condition of the things with which we are familiar in everyday experience. The case Aristotle puts up for saying that he exists depends on a theory of the physical universe which has long been discarded by astronomers, but there is nothing far-fetched about it in principle, as is shown by the fact that it is retained by sober writers like Thomas Aquinas and Locke. It is none the less an ideal example of the type of metaphysical reasoning which Kant condemns on the ground that it involves an illegitimate transition from the sensible to the supersensible sphere. If we agree with the Kantian characterization of metaphysics, outlined above, we shall have to say that Aristotle, in this part of his work at least, runs true to metaphysical form and promises us news from nowhere.

Happily this is not the end of the matter. If Aristotle seems in Book Λ of his *Metaphysics* to offer us only a tame version of the thought of Plato, a version which clearly owes as much to the *Laws* as the *Republic*, his standpoint in the rest of his work is very different. First philosophy is no longer conceived there as concerned with a special part of reality, namely 'things unseen', but is widened to become a universal study of substance or 'being as such'. And it turns out in practice that this somewhat mysterious phrase covers an enquiry into the proper way to take things already known, rather than a proposal to add to the sum of knowledge. Seen from this point of view, Aristotelian metaphysics has a logical status similar to that of materialism as just expounded, and indeed one of Aristotle's motives in discussing the subject would seem to have been to produce an alternative to materialism as he knew it in the work of Empedocles and Democritus.

Let me now try to elaborate and defend this position. Aristotle conceives his task as a metaphysician, much as the earliest Greek philosophers had, as being to say what there is in the world. In the work called the *Categories*, whose doctrines are presupposed throughout the *Metaphysics*, he distinguishes carefully between substantial and non-substantial being, along lines which have already been indicated in our discussion of materialism above. Substance is that to which things happen; a term expressing primary substance is one which can have predicates but cannot itself be predicated of anything further. Aristotle mentions individual men and horses as cases answering this description, and maintains that these 'exist independently', which they certainly do when compared with e.g. whiteness or being upside down. It looks from this as if the concept of substance were being applied very much in a commonsensical way, but further examination reveals that Aristotle is putting restrictions on its use. Not only does he deny the name of substance to certain continuants which apparently satisfy his logical prescription, such as individual rivers or individual statues, on the ground that they are more naturally taken as derivative (a statue, for example, being clay or metal shaped in a certain way): he makes a general connection between being a substance and existing by nature which is of the utmost importance for his whole scheme of thought. We must remember that the term 'nature' ($\phi\acute{\nu}\sigma\iota\varsigma$) had for the Greeks implications which it no longer has for us: it was connected in their thought with the ideas of growth and life. To speak of something as existing by nature, to someone who took this view, was to speak of it as existing as part of a scheme which had the appearance of being organized in the biological sense. It is entirely proper to ask of each of the constituents of such a scheme what function it is supposed to perform or, more crudely, what it is trying to be or do. And we find that these are precisely the terms in which Aristotle tends to think of the things to which he applies the name 'substance'. He sees his substances as each engaged in the process of becoming actually what it has it in itself to be, or again as striving to realize a certain form which it shares with others of its kind. He even applies this analysis to the four elements, earth, air, fire and water, at least two of which strike us as solidly material and inanimate, but which Aristotle thinks of as each seeking its natural place in the cosmos.

To make sense of Aristotle's metaphysics we have to take his doctrine of substance along with his doctrine of the four causes, which itself connects closely with the linked distinctions potentiality/ actuality and matter/form. The not very aptly named doctrine of the four causes is best seen as offering a way, or perhaps one should say an interconnected set of ways, of explaining both why things are what they are and why they change as they do. The notions of material and formal causation help us to understand things from the static point of view: we learn something about a person, to give a modern example, if we are told first something about his natural disposition and inherited tendencies, and then something about his character. We consider here both the matter out of which his personality is shaped and the form impressed on it, and there is no doubt that the whole procedure is, or can be, explanatory: in one sense at least we understand why the man is as he is after applying it. The notions of final and efficient causation are intended to make change intelligible. Final causes are, quite simply, ends or purposes: to ask for the final cause of a process is to enquire into the purpose which it serves. It is characteristic of Aristotle to see every process as purposive, though it should be added that he takes the term 'purpose' in a wide sense, according to which anything which performs a function could be said to have a purpose. The teleology here involved has been sometimes described as 'unconscious'; it is the sort of teleology appealed to by the physiologist when he speaks of the function of an organ, or by the zoologist when he says that an animal changes colour in order to escape detection by its enemies. Efficient causes as understood by Aristotle are less easy to explain. He believed, in effect, that not only was it the case that in every change form was being imposed upon matter, but further that it was a necessary condition of the change's coming about that the same sort of form should be embodied in the agent initiating the change. Thus, to take Aristotle's favourite example, the form of man had to be embodied in the male parent for the embryo to take it on and emerge as human. The main interest of this doctrine perhaps lies in the light it throws on the stringency of Aristotle's requirements in a scientific explanation (the notion of necessary connection involved is one of peculiar intimacy), but it also illustrates his tendency to make the notion of form his key concept in interpreting the world.

If we ask where Aristotle found these ideas, two sources can be suggested. One is reflection on his experience as a biologist, a capacity in which he exercised himself from an early stage of his career (his father was a doctor). Aristotle was deeply suspicious of attempts to explain biological phenomena in mechanistic terms; he knew, for example, of the possibility of natural selection, which had been suggested in a crude form by Empedocles, but rejected it as involving too many incredible coincidences. His fourfold scheme of causation is built on ideas to which a non-mechanistic, common-sense biologist would naturally appeal, and applies to biological phenomena more readily than elsewhere. It may, however, have been derived from reflection on a different range of happenings, namely men's activities in making things. Aristotle often exemplified the antithesis of matter and form by talking about the sculptor shaping bronze or marble or the builder turning wood and stone into a house. His attempt to show that, in the ideal explanation, final, formal and efficient causes coincide is most successful here: form must be present first in the shape of a plan in the builder's mind, then as the end towards which the whole is directed, finally as the structure which the finished product embodies. As Kant saw, there are important differences between the concept of purpose as it applies to human technical activities and the same concept as it applies in the description of living things: we in fact strain language when we describe organisms as 'purposes of nature'. But the chances are that Aristotle was unaware of these subtleties, and thus that a choice between the two suggested sources would have struck him as unimportant. It is notable that he passes, without showing any awareness of incongruity, from talking about things like building to talking about health in the body as formal and final cause; he clearly thought the same analysis applied to both cases. And indeed he would have considered it one of its chief merits that it did so, since it thus became possible to bring widely divergent phenomena under a single interpretative scheme.

We are now in a position to characterize this second aspect of Aristotle's metaphysics more exactly. Although the prominence given to the concept of substance means that it is formally an ontology, a doctrine of what there is, the way Aristotle works it out shows that he was primarily concerned to give a unitary account of experience as a whole. Thanks to his possession of the concepts of matter and form, the notions of potentiality and actuality and the fourfold scheme of causation he thought himself in a position to throw light on whatever occurs anywhere. He certainly never meant to restrict the application of these ideas to the sphere of biology, but attempted to extend their use backwards into what we now call physics and chemistry, and forwards into psychology, morals and politics. And though, not surprisingly, his success in these different spheres was unequal, his achievement is not to be measured entirely by his ability to deal with individual problems. Certainly when we read Aristotle we are impressed with the many enlightening things he has to say, on subjects like psychology and politics for instance. But we are also impressed by the way he sustains a single point of view over many different fields; the facts that he has this point of view, and has clear ideas about how to apply it, are important in themselves. That Aristotle was ignorant on many points of fact, and consequently misapplied his ideas, is not in itself proof that his system is misconceived; the possibility remains, after all, that a modern Aristotelian will be able to apply them better. Nor is Aristotle decisively refuted when it is shown that there are whole areas of enquiry in which modern thinking runs on lines which are different from his. The fact that formal and final causes have been banished from physical science no more invalidates Aristotelianism than the corresponding fact that they remain very much part of the thought of historians and novelists invalidates its rival materialism. It is not even certain, indeed, that the banishment is total or permanent: as Whitehead and others have argued, the mechanical outlook of classical physics is not fully sustained in its modern counterpart, with the result that a modified form of Aristotelianism, in which the concept of substance is replaced by that of function, may be valid even in this field. But it must be added that Aristotelians cannot be satisfied indefinitely with the contemplation of this bare possibility; the longer they remain without a convincing account of the concepts of physical science, the less conviction their metaphysics will carry. Even a metaphysician cannot exist on promises alone.

The implications of these remarks for the question of the status of metaphysical theories and assertions will be the subject of a later discussion. In the meantime we must bring this brief survey of Aristotle's ideas to an end by asking how his two conceptions of metaphysics are related. It has been argued that Aristotle began his philosophical career as a Platonist but developed increasingly strong empirical interests as he proceeded, and this hypothesis can be taken as broadly correct, even if not substantiated in all its details. But it will not follow that the conception of metaphysics as the science of pure form, or 'theology' as Aristotle himself describes it, can be set aside as the product of his youth, leaving the alternative view to represent his maturity. There is no denying that Book Λ of the *Metaphysics* has every appearance of being separate from the rest of that somewhat heterogeneous work, but this in itself does not make it early, and indeed the astronomical passages it includes suggest that some parts of it date from the very end of Aristotle's career. We have every reason to think that he believed in the Unmoved Mover to the last. Nor is it at all surprising that he should have done so, apart from the key position which that entity occupied in his account of the physical world. In his ethics, too, Aristotle moved far from the simple Platonism he had expounded in his early dialogues; he developed an illuminating series of ethical concepts of his own built round the very unPlatonic notion of 'practical reason', but he continued to say with Plato that the best life is the life of pure contemplation. If the *Magna Moralia* is genuine we have three versions of Aristotle's thoughts about morals, and the doctrine of the supremacy of the contemplative life appears in each one of them. Similarly in his psychology Aristotle began with something like the two-substance theory of the *Phaedo* and eventually came to think that the soul should be conceived as the form of the body, a view which would strictly imply that its separate existence is a logical absurdity. Yet he stated in a passage in the *De motu animalium* whose authenticity is not in question that the 'active reason' at least comes from without and is immortal. It may be regrettable that he could not shake off this relic of Platonism, but it seems to be a fact that he did not do so. And it seems likely in the same way that the Platonic conception of metaphysics survived in his thought alongside the very different conception we have tried to outline, the idea of substance being the formal link between the two. Because he believed in 'sensible' as well as 'insensible' substance Aristotle could elaborate what is in effect a metaphysics of experience, a doctrine of how to take familiar things. A modern critic might well see this as ruling out belief in things unseen on the Platonic pattern, but there is no evidence that Aristotle, who after all continued to believe in the intuitive powers of reason, ever took that view. On the contrary, he held that things seen can be explained only if we presume the existence of things unseen. To lay exclusive stress on either of our alternatives would accordingly be seriously mistaken.

5

Metaphysics without Ontology

1. Points of comparison in the systems discussed: (a) metaphysics and common sense

WE CAN now proceed to a comparison of the three metaphysical systems we have discussed in outline, with the particular object of clarifying the alternative to what we are, perhaps unfairly, calling the Platonic conception of metaphysics. Before noticing any points of difference, it will be useful to mention some respects in which the three are in agreement. Each of them claims to reveal final and fundamental truth; each works with the antithesis of reality and appearance, and professes to tell us what things are really like, as opposed to how they merely appear to be; each in consequence involves a rejection of beliefs or procedures which non-philosophers, or 'common sense', take to be entirely in order. All three assume that it is both possible and desirable to produce a general theory of reality, and rely very largely on argument, as opposed to observation and experiment, in setting up such a theory.

I shall take it that the account of Plato given in Chapter 2 above is full and explicit enough to make further discussion of these points unnecessary as far as he is concerned. That they apply to materialism and Aristotelianism (except so far as it reproduces Platonism) may seem less obvious. It is however clear on reflection that the partisans of both these views conceive their task as being to inform us of the real nature of the world, and that their first move in recommending their position must be to sow dissatisfaction with everyday or commonsense beliefs.

Materialism, as we saw, can be taken either as asserting that, contrary to first appearances, matter alone exists as substance, or as maintaining that whatever occurs can be satisfactorily explained in scientific terms only. The formulations differ, but the underlying claim to reveal fundamental truth is as clear as in the case of Plato. And while a materialist can scarcely be expected to cast doubt on the evidence of the senses on the model of a Plato or a Descartes, he is committed, as I tried to bring out, to rejecting or depreciating ways of thinking whose propriety and importance are as obvious to the common man as is the proposition that there is such a thing as sense-knowledge. He must, in effect, argue that the distinction between doing something for a reason and being caused to do it is at best superficial, the truth being that everything *really* happens as a result of the operation of causes. And this position carries with it an altered attitude to much else that forms part of our accepted ways of thought: for example, to all the elaborate procedures of justification and excuse, with the associated talk of threats, provocation and inducement, which are employed so widely in the fields of law and morals. A materialist can hardly take these with the seriousness with which they are treated by lawyers and moralists, if only because he cannot accept the notion of responsibility on which they depend. He need not dispense entirely with the vocabulary of praise and blame; he can say that there are certain things which ought or ought not to have been done. But he will use this language, if he is consistent, with restricted implications, as we do when we apply it to dogs or small children, regarding it in effect as a form of pressure which will influence their future behaviour rather than have any true relevance to what they have done in the past. Similarly he will refuse to draw the sharp distinctions which remain very much a part of unsophisticated legal and moral thought between punishing a person who is guilty and treating a man who is physically or mentally sick and therefore unable to help himself; that all offenders are sick will not strike him as a paradox. As for the law itself, he will be inclined to pay less attention to its formal structure than to its social background, and to sympathize with the sociological approaches of American jurists rather than the more narrowly professional methods of their colleagues in Britain.

It seems clear from this that materialism involves as violent a break with conventionally accepted ways of thinking as does

Platonism, though the break takes a very different form. Can the same be said of the metaphysics of Aristotle? Mr Strawson has recently described Aristotle as practising 'descriptive' rather than 'revisionary' metaphysics, meaning to suggest thereby that he intended to make explicit the concepts fundamental to ordinary ways of thinking rather than to propose their replacement by an entirely different set of ideas. But though it is true that much of Aristotle's work is descriptive in this sense, it would be wrong to underemphasize the distinctive character of Aristotelianism. As I have tried to show, the concept of substance employed by Aristotle is not identical with the commonsense conception, according to which any continuing thing—anything which would be thought to have a history—is regarded as substantial. Aristotle modifies this conception by confining substance to what exists by nature, thus opening the way for universal application of his fourfold scheme of causation. The fact that each of the 'causes' is appealed to in various contexts in everyday thought should not distract our attention from the equally firm fact that Aristotle wanted to apply them all everywhere, and believed that by so doing we could arrive at a true account of things. Becoming an Aristotelian certainly involves less intellectual readjustment than becoming a Platonist or a materialist, but it would be false to imagine that it could be entirely painless. It demands a sustained imaginative effort which is by no means easy for people living today, even though it must have been somewhat easier for Aristotle's own contemporaries. And this fact in itself shows that there is no difference of principle between the metaphysics of Aristotle and the other metaphysical theories we have studied.

2. *Points of comparison in the systems discussed:* (b) *materialism and the supersensible*

Let us leave the question of the points on which our three systems are in agreement and pass to those over which they differ. One which is supremely important concerns the alleged connection between metaphysics and the supersensible. In expounding Platonism, and still more in outlining the standard criticisms of metaphysics in Chapter 3, we paid particular attention to the antithesis between things seen and things unseen, objects of the senses and objects of the intellect. We took Plato's demand that men should abandon belief for knowledge as what it literally seemed to be, an injunction to turn their attention from the familiar everyday world, which proved on examination to be full of contradiction and therefore merely apparent, to the real world of Forms which lay behind it and could be grasped not by the senses but by the intellect. In so doing we saw metaphysics as claiming to give us information of a kind which was at once specially certain and specially important. It was from this point that we went on to develop the Kantian and Positivist criticisms, which maintain that the claim is entirely without foundation.

Is it true that materialism professes to offer us knowledge of the supersensible? It was certainly represented as doing so by the Positivists, who supported their position by an argument on the following lines. The materialist says that nothing exists except matter. If he means this to be an empirical statement, i.e. if he is taking matter to be the genus of which wood and stone are species, then he is saying something which would generally be judged to be false, if only because of the common conviction that states of consciousness cannot inhere in things material. It follows that he must intend the statement to be taken differently, and must be supposing 'matter' to be the name, not of something palpable and familiar, but of a remote kind of stuff which is not accessible to immediate experience. The matter he postulates is thus identical with the matter Berkeley supposed Locke to have accepted, and the case for disregarding it as the product of confusion is as strong as the parallel case against Platonic Forms. Both being beyond the range of human experience, we simply do not know what either might be like, and therefore use words to no purpose when we profess to talk about them.

The short reply to this attempt to involve the materialist in an impossible dilemma is that he need choose neither of the alternatives proffered. He need not make the choice because he can claim that he is not advancing a factual thesis of any sort. He is saying how things must be taken if we are to make sense of them, not professing to inform us about what there is in the world, despite the misleading way in which his main contention is commonly formulated. He is wanting to urge on us a point of view, the point of view which maintains that science alone has the answers. And in putting this forward he certainly has no reason to commit himself to the existence of a world of any kind beyond the range of the senses, for his whole object is with making sense of this world.

Does this mean that a materialist is really an empirical scientist of a peculiar kind? The identification is easy to make, but nevertheless quite mistaken. Materialism as I have explained it is not itself a scientific thesis; it is a doctrine which asserts the omnicompetence of science. A materialist makes a pronouncement about science, but does not necessarily engage in any form of scientific activity himself. The results which scientists establish are of vital concern when we come to make up our minds about materialism, yet it would be wrong to think that materialists simply repeat those results. What they add can be brought out if we say that, whereas scientists assert their conclusions as true, materialists see them as embodying *the* truth on the subject in question. Now it is clear that to make a claim about the comprehensive and convincing character of scientific conclusions is in no sense to contribute to those conclusions. It is equally clear that it is not to say anything about the supersensible.

The key proposition of materialism regarded as a metaphysics of experience might be put in the form: it is out of the question that there should be anything that cannot be satisfactorily explained in scientific terms. It should be obvious in the first place that this is not an empirical proposition: no amount of scrutiny of the evidence could establish a principle of such unrestricted generality. We can discover by examining facts what the world is like, but not that it would be absurd not to take it in a certain way. It should be obvious again that it is not an analytic proposition: no breach of the laws of logic is involved in its denial. A man who rejects the thesis of materialism does not involve himself in self-contradiction, even though his position may strike supporters of that philosophy as absurd. The alleged absurdity of the denial is a different kind of absurdity from logical absurdity, just as the alleged necessity of the materialist thesis is a different kind of necessity from logical necessity. We can bring in the words 'synthetic *a priori*' if we are looking for a label for a proposition of this sort, and they are appropriate in so far as it is at once significant (non-tautological) and necessary. But if we do this it must be with the proviso that we are not professing to deal here with a necessary truth of fact, but rather with something which has the force of a prescription. A proposition of this sort, if it can rightly be called a proposition, is neither read out of experience as is an everyday empirical truth nor established, as opponents of metaphysics have long said that metaphysicians must claim as the only alternative, by an act of intellectual intuition. Showing that intellectual intuition is unreal for human beings will accordingly be without bearing on the validity of this form of metaphysics.

To repeat and underline the main point: materialism on this view of the matter is not a doctrine about what is to be found in the world, still less out of it. A materialist does not have to claim to know any existence propositions of which his opponents are ignorant; what he has to claim is ability to get into perspective, or understand, things with which everyone either is or could be familiar. It is true that the materialist position carries with it the denial of certain existence claims which have been made by other philosophers, for instance the Aristotelian claim that there exist purely spiritual beings. But the materialist can make this denial without having to presuppose any special insight into the Beyond: he makes it because he is convinced that the facts do not warrant any such assumption, in the same way as most of us deny the existence of fairies because we see that the facts do not justify our assuming it. He could, if he chose, stop short of absolute denial of a claim like Aristotle's, and say only that there was nothing to be said for it; to counter him, an opponent would have to point to *phenomena* which materialism leaves unexplained.

3. *Further cases considered*

Aristotle. I shall now take it as established that materialism constitutes an exception to the 'news from nowhere' view of metaphysics: it is neither necessary nor even more than superficially plausible to take it as offering us information about supersensible reality. The question then arises whether it is an isolated exception, or whether other metaphysical systems can be properly interpreted on similar lines. The first thing that needs to be said in this connection is that any form of metaphysics which professes to offer an alternative to materialism must share its logical status. We mentioned above that one of Aristotle's motives in putting forward a 'first philosophy' was to state an alternative to theories like those of Empedocles and Democritus, who had argued respectively that everything could be satisfactorily explained in purely mechanical terms and that what really existed was only atoms and void. Since Aristotle was concerned to refute both of these propositions, it must be allowed that formally even this part of his philosophy includes a number of ontological assertions as well as a series of recommendations about how to take what occurs. But it is perhaps not wholly extravagant, even if it might have seemed strange to Aristotle himself, to maintain that the former is really subordinate to the latter, and to see the essence of Aristotelianism as consisting in the urging of a distinctive view of the world. It is this impression, after all, which we take away from reading his many-sided writings: we are struck by the spectacle of a man who is entirely clear in his own mind about first principles, and is ready to apply them, with some show of success as it turns out, to the most diverse groups of phenomena. If we want to estimate the force of Aristotle's ideas, we have no need to pay attention to what he says or implies about existence: it is the terms in which he proposed to interpret what exists which matter.

I have already emphasized that it is quite wrong historically to represent Aristotle as being exclusively concerned with sensible substance; his belief in pure form cannot be dismissed. But though this means that the account given above cannot be complete, it does not discredit it entirely. At the lowest estimate there is an important aspect of Aristotle's thought which answers to the view we are considering. Nor could it be argued that, even when he departs from this conception of metaphysics, Aristotle is a straightforward advocate of the Platonic alternative. He nowhere shows that unhealthy preoccupation with the supersensible for its own sake which is found in some forms of eastern metaphysics and involves a contempt for the things of this world. Aristotle's motive in postulating things supersensible is to explain the here and now, not to dismiss it as unreal. It might even be held that this kind of belief in the supersensible can be made empirically respectable, on the ground of its similarity to scientific belief in unexperienceable entities, but this possibility must be reserved for later discussion.

Leibniz. I turn now from Aristotle to his modern counterpart Leibniz. First appearances suggest that Leibniz should be classed with Plato as belonging to the 'news from nowhere' school. His philosophy begins, like that of Descartes from which it is here derived, by casting doubt on the evidence of the senses; it proceeds to the assertion that the real stuff of the universe is of a spiritual nature and can be grasped by the intellect alone. Monads are, as Leibniz puts it, the 'true atoms of nature', and the operation of monads cannot be discerned by experimental or observational means. Kant, who took Leibniz to be the very type of a metaphysical philosopher, and who had studied him deeply if not always very sympathetically, certainly reads him in this way: he takes Leibniz to be working with the Platonic antithesis of a sensible and an intelligible world, and to be declaring that the latter is true reality. Yet it is notable that Leibniz had at one time felt the attraction of materialism, which he later decided was an incoherent and therefore impossible philosophy; and there seems little doubt that one consideration which recommended his monadology in his own eyes was its ability to deal with phenomena which mechanists could not satisfactorily explain, especially biological phenomena. As an alternative to materialism, the philosophy of Leibniz would be a doctrine of how to take familiar facts, not a revelation of a fresh set of them.

It may be that we are partly precluded from seeing it in this way by the misleading associations of some of Leibniz's own remarks. He speaks of monads as 'the elements of things' and again as 'simples': the implication of this seems to be that if we could only get down to what things are made of we should come to ultimate subjects of predication whose nature is pure spirituality, if any meaning can be attached to that phrase. This would make a monad simple in the way in which Russell thought that a sense-datum of red was simple. But it is quite evident when we come to read Leibniz that he never meant to subscribe to a view of this sort. A monad, for all its alleged simplicity, is a complex entity, as is shown by the fact that it is intended to embrace a variety of phases; it is a unity in diversity, as a person is a unity in diversity. To speak of the monad which constitutes Julius Caesar is not to refer to a mysterious something, undetectable by the senses but immediately apprehensible from within, which supposedly remained constant throughout Caesar's life and constituted the real *him*. Hume pretended that believers in spiritual substance were committed to some such view, but there is nothing to show that Leibniz so much as contemplated it. A more charitable interpretation of his doctrine would see the monad as an organizing concept of a higher logical order than those we use in describing particular actions or events; to say that what we are really concerned with in a given situation is the operations of a monad is to suggest that we should see the situation in a certain light. The term 'monad' on this view would be the name of a complex particular, as 'revolution' is the name of a complex particular; a monad could not be singled out for attention, even by the eye of the soul. As we shall see presently, a similar account can be given of other metaphysical concepts, including Bradley's concept of the Absolute.

I am not saying that Leibniz himself explicitly formulated this view, though I think it is clear that he could have held it, nor should I wish to maintain that his whole metaphysics could be presented as a metaphysics of experience. The fact that he refurbished the traditional proofs of God's existence and stuck to the Christian conception of God as a being who was all spirit is enough to show the impossibility of that. The system of Leibniz is in this respect like that of Aristotle: in each case there is an existential commitment, all-important in the eyes of the author, which cannot be reconciled with what might be called an immanentist reading of what is being said. But though this admission is certainly vital, it does not take away from the fact that we can make sense, up to a point at least, even of such unpromising material as this by taking it as a series of recommendations about the here and now instead of as news from nowhere. That Leibniz himself was careful to indicate the experiential basis of some of his main concepts may be taken as further evidence in favour of this view.

Hegel. It is to Hegel and his followers that we must look for purer examples of the revised type of metaphysics we are seeking to clarify. Hegel of course wrote with the classical criticisms of Hume and Kant before him, and certainly paid attention to the latter if not much to the former. He was in agreement with Kant over one point in particular: that if we distinguish between 'appearances', which are objects of the senses, and 'things in themselves', which are supposed to be known by a superior intellectual faculty, knowledge of things in themselves will turn out to be impossible. But he regarded this not as a fatal blow to metaphysics, but simply as evidence that its nature had been radically misconceived.

Hegel was quite innocent of the yearning of which Kant had spoken to pass from the sensible to the supersensible sphere; he was not himself in the least other-worldly, but was passionately interested in all sorts of things in the everyday world, as the wide variety of his writings makes clear. He was concerned, amongst other things, with questions about religion, problems of art, issues in ethics and politics, both practical and theoretical, and with the status of the concepts of natural science and their internal and external relationships; he looked to philosophy to provide him with what amounted to a series of master concepts in terms of which to make sense of this highly diverse material. But, contrary to popular belief, he did not think of the philosopher as fetching up these master concepts from the depths of his own consciousness: philosophy was to begin from concern with things empirical, as it actually did in Hegel's own case, and must test its conclusions continually by seeking to apply them to empirical data. It was the mark of an inadequate philosophy to be at once unsatisfyingly abstract and rough in its application; such a system could be said to present us only with an account of 'appearances', not with truth about 'reality'. But it will be noticed that the antithesis between appearance and reality is not here taken as it was in the Platonic tradition to which Kant subscribed: the terms are not applied to two distinct sorts of entity, but to the same entities described less and more adequately. It is true that Hegel added that the concepts of an inadequate system of metaphysics would prove to be internally incoherent, which seems to suggest that the merits of a metaphysician could be decided by considerations of pure logic. But though he was notorious for seeing 'contradictions' everywhere, except perhaps in his own theories, it is not clear that he took the word in a purely logical way. A theory can be said to be contradictory in a loose sense when it fails to measure up to facts or promises more than it can perform, and Hegel may well have had this loose sense sometimes in mind. At any rate in treating his predecessors he does not confine himself to questions of consistency, but considers the acceptability of their theories from an altogether broader point of view.

Bradley. I shall be dealing at length in a later chapter with the origin of Hegel's metaphysics, and accordingly shall not consider his system further at this point. Instead, I should like to turn briefly to examine the metaphysical theory of F. H. Bradley, widely reputed to have been an English Hegelian despite certain disclaimers on his own part, and thought of by many analytic philosophers as a typical purveyor of news from nowhere. I hope to show that this characterization is definitely incorrect.

'The "individual" apart from the community', wrote Bradley in his celebrated essay on 'My Station and its Duties' in *Ethical Studies,* 'is not anything real.'[1] It is a pity that Bradley's critics did not pay more attention to this use of the term 'real'. For it is clear when we reflect on the matter that Bradley was not meaning here to assert that there never has in fact been an individual who has lived entirely apart from society, or indeed to make any statement about what exists. He was concerned rather with the tenability of a certain concept, a concept which struck him as a product of vicious abstraction. If you strip off from a person what he owes to heredity on the one hand and family and social environment on the other, the argument was, you are left with nothing significant at all: an 'individual' of this sort is entirely unintelligible. Bradley's purpose in deploying the argument was to dispute the correctness of the approach to politics made by J. S. Mill and the Philosophical Radicals, which seemed to him both practically and theoretically objectionable. He was wanting to maintain that this approach rests on an assumption which cannot be rationally justified.

Similarly when Bradley as a metaphysician said that time is not real but merely 'qualifies appearances', he was not intending to deny

1. 2nd edition, p. 173.

any facts but rather to challenge the propriety of a certain way of taking facts. Moore in his well-known essay on 'The Conception of Reality' thought he could refute Bradley here by the simple expedient of producing temporal statements which no one in his senses would dispute, e.g. 'All sorts of things happened last week'. But Bradley clearly never meant to question the correctness of individual statements of this kind. He did not doubt the applicability of the temporal way of thinking, or indeed its necessity at a certain level; what seemed to him uncertain was whether this whole way of thinking was ultimately coherent. He argued—whether rightly or wrongly does not matter for our present purposes—that the notion of time involves the two incompatible notions of continuity and discreteness, and was accordingly such that it could not be predicated of reality, reality being harmonious and free from contradiction. Many of Bradley's readers have interpreted him as working with a two-world view here, but it is fairer to see him as having accepted the Hegelian way of taking the antithesis of appearance and reality explained above. It was with the relative appropriateness of rival conceptual schemes that he was concerned, and indeed it is only on this basis that we can make any sense of his talk of *degrees* of truth and reality.

If we look at Bradley's main work *Appearance and Reality* with these considerations in mind I suggest that we can make sense of it on the following lines. In the first part of the book Bradley is examining a number of familiar metaphysical theories: a version of materialism which tries to explain discrepancies in immediate experience in terms of the old distinction between primary and secondary qualities in bodies; the metaphysics of common sense, which takes ideas like space, time and causality to be each of them in order just as it is; a version of the 'spiritualist' rival to materialism which finds contradictions in the concepts of natural science but believes that the soul at least is palpable reality. Bradley argues that none of these can pass muster, not even the last which, as it turns out, puts its trust in a concept whose ambiguities are monumental (those who accused Bradley of being 'tender-minded' can scarcely have read his chapters on the soul). These discussions, whose results are wholly negative, occupy something like a quarter of the work.

In the remaining chapters, which form a separate book under the encouraging heading 'Reality', Bradley describes and argues for an alternative and, in his view, altogether more satisfactory way of characterizing things. Reality, according to the view here expounded, is to be seen as a single self-differentiating system whose nature is experience; it is to be thought of as including whatever appears, but including it in such a way as to show it to be 'harmonious'. Conviction that these are in fact the best terms in which to take reality came to Bradley from reflection on a particular experience, which he called the experience of feeling. At the level of feeling, which underlies that of reflective or discursive thought, we sense the world as a unity in diversity; separate elements are not picked out at this level, but the conviction that they are there to be separated out, i.e. that we are not dealing with bare, undifferentiated unity, is overwhelming. It was Bradley's view that reflective thought actually carries out the separation but carries it out too thoroughly, since it hardens the elements separated into supposedly independent entities. All human thinking is bedevilled by abstraction and false hypostatization of this kind, but the metaphysician must strive to overcome it as far as he can and so to reconstitute the innocence which existed before the Fall, though at a level above that of relational thinking instead of below it. Bradley was convinced that failure here was certain, since, as Kant had argued, the human intellect has no intuitive powers, but he did not draw the conclusion that we should eschew metaphysics. He argued, however, that the most we could do was sketch the lines on which a satisfactory metaphysical view might be worked out; to ask us to fill in the details was in effect to ask for the impossible.

I shall not discuss the special problems raised by this last point, but shall proceed at once to comment on the concept with which Bradley's name is most familiarly associated by modern students of philosophy, the concept of the Absolute. It is notorious that Bradley had much to say of this strange entity, and the temptation to take it as a mythical monster, a denizen of an imaginary world lying beyond the range of ordinary experience, is very strong. I think myself that it was unfortunate that Bradley ever used this term, which he derived from Hegel and ultimately from Kant, in view of the misleading suggestion that it names a special sort of particular or functions as a definite description singling out a particular member of a class. But I do not see how anyone can read Bradley attentively and continue under this misapprehension.

'The Absolute', despite the presence of the definite article, is not the name of a particular which can be contrasted with other particulars; it is the term Bradley applies to the whole of reality considered as a single, self-differentiating system, precisely the sort of unity in diversity which Bradley believed it to be. To speak of the properties of the Absolute is to speak of what is real as opposed to what is apparent. Bradley is at one with all other metaphysicians in refusing to accept experience at its face value; he holds as strongly as any that the task of metaphysics is to characterize reality. But he differs from some other speculative thinkers and agrees with Spinoza in holding that there cannot be a plurality of things which are ultimately real, and it is for this reason that he employs the otherwise puzzling phrase, '*the* real'. For him, 'the real' and 'the Absolute' are one and the same. But, as he is never tired of emphasizing, the Absolute is nothing apart from its appearances, and this not in the sense that it is causally dependent on them, as an eminent personage might be nothing apart from his advisers because he depends on their help, but in a more straightforward logical sense. The Absolute apart from its appearances would be like a political organization without members or officers, or an economic system in which there were no economic agents and no economic transactions. It would, in short, make no sense to speak of the Absolute in contrast with its appearances, since the whole point of introducing the concept is to co-ordinate appearances.

This is not to say that 'the Absolute' is merely another name for the sum of appearances. Bradley speaks frequently of things being 'transformed' in the Absolute; the implication of this terminology is that the world is very different from what it seems to be. Reality may be nothing apart from appearances, but it is equally clear to Bradley that appearances are not real 'in their character as presented'. Finite truths are only partial truths, each carrying with it suggestions of error; what they say needs to be re-expressed, its content being expanded until it is finally all-embracing. The final result will seem strange or even unintelligible to those who have not felt the metaphysical urge and tried for themselves to arrive at a satisfactory system of ideas. But, strange or not, the fact remains that it is an attempt to cover precisely the same data as are dealt with by the more familiar methods of common sense. It seeks to give a coherent account of appearances, not to explain them away or to divert attention from them by beguiling us with news from nowhere. To give conviction to his philosophy, Bradley needs to make out both its negative and its positive sides: he has to show that the ways of thinking he discards really are unable to perform what they promise, and he has to make his own alternative to them clear and compulsive. It is possible that he falls down on one or other of these, if not on both. His vision of the world as an integrated and self-integrating system was certainly not shared by opponents like Russell, who found his arguments about relations all falling within a wider whole merely mystifying and could make nothing of the appeal to feeling with which he supported them. His dismissal of the categories of common sense—thing and property, quality and relation, cause, activity, space and time—as being one and all inadequate for metaphysical purposes was thought to be grossly mistaken by Moore, whose view here is taken as orthodoxy by a great number of contemporary philosophers. It may be that the demand for a 'theory of first principles', as Bradley somewhere defines metaphysics, is mistaken in itself: that is a point I shall be taking up in a later chapter. Or even if it is not mistaken, it may be that Bradley has not supplied the kind of first principles that are wanted; an altogether different view, of the materialist type, for instance, might turn out to carry greater conviction. But to attack Bradley on these grounds is at least to treat him seriously; to pretend that his whole system can be set aside because none of us knows just what it would be like to be in the presence of the Absolute is merely to show logical ignorance. Even a metaphysician has a right to a fairer examination than that.

4. *Some provisional conclusions*

The examples we have considered seem to me to show decisively that being a metaphysician does not necessarily mean claiming ability to reveal truths about a world which lies beyond the reach of the senses. To put it crudely, you can practise metaphysics and still keep your feet firmly planted on the ground, since your concern as a metaphysician is with how to take what happens here and now. I do not say at this point that every metaphysical system can be represented in this way; the indications so far are rather that there are some, such as that of Plato, which fit the classical conception of the subject much better, and others which admit of either the classical or our revised type of interpretation, in each case at the cost of ignoring features which the author concerned considered to be vital. It remains true, none the less, that a major preoccupation of at least some of the most important metaphysicians has been to tell us how to take the scheme of things entire, which has meant in effect getting the things of this world into perspective.

These phrases are at best vague, and I must now do what I can to clarify them. Let me begin by saying that the metaphysicians with whom we are concerned, those who offer a metaphysics of experience, see their task as being to give a unitary account of whatever occurs. A unitary account, in this connection, is something more than a complete description, for the latter might be made from many points of view, without any question being raised about whether the points of view were compatible. To list all the propositions which would be accepted by common sense might produce such a complete description, but it would not amount to the construction of a metaphysics. The fundamental reason for this is that any metaphysics involves an element of explicit theory, whilst common sense is conspicuously untheoretical. The ordinary man switches without any feeling of incongruity from, say, the language of reasons to the language of causes, showing little or no awareness of the possibility that each may be applicable only if a certain theoretical claim is made good. Metaphysicians are by contrast professionally preoccupied with just such claims. It is their thesis both that the thought of the ordinary man is confused, since it rests on various assumptions which cannot be shown to be consistent, and that it can and should be replaced by a better way of thinking, in which everything is brought under a single explanatory scheme, clearly recognized and consciously applied. At least some of the theories we have examined would be said to exemplify such schemes, though it is obvious that no single metaphysician could allow final validity to more than one of them.

The 'unitary account' spoken of above is thus both descriptive and explanatory; it professes to cover both what there is and why it takes the form it does. How does it differ from the sort of account which could be expected of a scientist? In the first place by being more comprehensive, or by being comprehensive in a different way. As we saw before, a scientist may claim that there is nothing in the world which could be properly exempted from scientific scrutiny without wishing to suggest that scientists alone have the right to be heard; *qua* scientist he will aim at producing truth, but not necessarily the whole truth. Metaphysicians have no comparable modesty: it is their boast, whether well or ill founded, to be able to reveal *the* truth about reality.

This means that metaphysics is of its nature a higher-order activity than natural (or for that matter social) science, and this is a point of some importance. It is a higher-order activity, in the first place, because the metaphysician must take account of other approaches besides the scientific, even if he finally decides that it is the scientist who has the important answers. He must, for example, consider the point of view of the religious man as well as that of the social scientist or psychologist who seems to explain religion away, and enquire carefully into the assumptions upon which each party proceeds, giving reasons for his final preference instead of simply asserting it dogmatically. A scientist can afford to work within a framework of ideas which he accepts without question, but metaphysics has always pretended to be self-critical.

It is true that there are difficulties in justifying this pretension— the 'unhypothetical first beginning' of which Plato spoke has an unhappy tendency to turn either into a logical truism from which nothing follows or into a trick proposition like the Cartesian *cogito ergo sum*[1]—but the point about the difference of levels remains valid. And it has the further implication that whereas the scientist pronounces directly on the value of hypotheses which purport to explain particular phenomena, metaphysicians are concerned with such hypotheses only indirectly, in so far as they may be considered to have put their confidence in a particular *type* of explanation. We saw when examining materialism that a man could assert the omnicompetence of science without having to

1. On this see the following chapter.

make any scientific contributions himself; giving scientific answers is one thing, thinking that the scientist has all the answers quite another. The latter position in fact involves making a judgment about the supreme value of seeking scientific explanations, and while this could be affected by scientific successes or failures, it would not be affected by them directly.

Another way of putting this point is to say that scientists and metaphysicians will differ in their attitude to facts. For the scientist facts are everything: if his theories cannot account for them, they must in the end be discarded. It is true that the complex propositions of advanced scientific theory are not open to direct empirical confutation in the straightforward way empiricist philosophers once supposed: the concern of scientists with 'pure cases' means that they can afford to ignore irregular or accidental happenings. But there is, even so, a severe limit to the lengths to which this policy can be taken. A scientific theory which *persistently* failed to fit the facts must be regarded as having broken down. Now meta-physicians are also sensitive to the pressure of facts, but in a different way. It is often highly important for them that a certain fact has been explained or remains unexplained, and much of their activity consists in pointing to facts which their own view stresses and which, as it seems to them, are inadequately dealt with by their opponents. But if it were suggested, as in fact it sometimes is, that metaphysical theories too must be open to empirical confutation, it would be only fair to say that few or no such confutations have been achieved. The explanation of this is to be found, I suggest, in the metaphysician's remoteness from actual empirical enquiry: because he does not have to produce explanations himself, he can always live for a time on hope. He can feel confident, that is to say, that an awkward fact which has not yet been explained on lines which fit his theory will in time be explained in just this way.[1] But if the required explanation fails to appear after prolonged search, only a dishonest metaphysician could continue to hold his theory with unimpaired conviction.

In discussing materialism above we suggested that a way to

1. Compare e.g. the discussions between materialists and anti-materi-alists about whether there is an absolute gulf between organic and inorganic matter.

formulate its main contention would be to claim that it is out of the question that there should be anything that cannot be satisfactorily explained in scientific terms. This formula has the advantage of making clear that materialism is a view about how to take things; it also shows the concern of the materialist, typical of this kind of metaphysics, with defining the bounds of sense and nonsense, or again with prescribing a framework inside which empirical enquiries can be most profitably pursued. Parallel formulae could be produced for rival metaphysical theories; that for Aristotelianism, for example, might run: it is out of the question that there should be anything that does not serve a purpose. We could say if we liked that the formulae given represented the basic assumptions or 'major premises' of materialism and Aristotelianism respectively. We could also, at a pinch, describe them as synthetic *a priori* principles, though if we did so there would surely be no temptation to think of them as constituting necessary truths of *fact*.

We saw that Plato equated knowing with exercising a sort of intellectual vision, and drew the conclusion that metaphysical truth could be experienced but not communicated. It is important to realize that insight has a place even in our revised form of metaphysics. At the centre of each of the systems we have considered there might be said to lie a certain intuition, an imaginative picture which constitutes the metaphysician's primary insight; it is from this that he starts and to this that he constantly returns. Thus at the centre of materialism there lies the picture of reality as a vast, unthinking machine, and anyone who is to feel the force of this system must grasp and appreciate that picture. Similarly in Hegelianism the central thought is perhaps to be found in the notion of a person's becoming more truly himself by triumphing over circumstances which at first seem alien to his personality, but are later seen to be necessary for its full development; however unlikely it may sound, Hegel tried to give an overall reading of experience in terms of this idea. It would of course be quite absurd to suggest that insight of this kind constitutes the whole stuff of metaphysics; if this were so there would clearly be no important difference between metaphysics and philosophical poetry. A metaphysician is, on any estimate, more intellectual than a poet, in so far as at least one of his tasks is to give conceptual expression to his primary idea; he needs not only to have a central vision, but further to frame a scheme of concepts in terms of which to give the unitary account of which we spoke above. He needs, in fact, to argue as well as to have a vision. But it is not absurd to maintain that vision is important as well as argument when it comes to appreciating and criticizing metaphysical thought. A critic who persistently refuses to see the world through the eyes of the metaphysician he is attacking will often fail to understand his arguments, or will direct his criticism against points which his opponent thinks quite unimportant. We have only to remember Russell's criticisms of Bradley, or for that matter Bradley's criticisms of Russell's Logical Atomism, to see the truth of this.

These remarks should not be misunderstood. It is one thing to enter into a metaphysician's point of view, and quite another to endorse it. If the understanding of a metaphysical system demanded that we should actively subscribe to the metaphysician's central insight, criticism of such a system could at best be internal and relative. It is true that much good criticism in metaphysics answers this description, but it does not follow that no other sort of criticism is possible. As I shall try to establish in detail later,[1] there are ways of assessing metaphysical points of view and of estimating their adequacy, though they should be compared not with the knock-down procedures followed in mathematics and the physical sciences, but rather with the looser types of argument appealed to in the criticism of literature and the arts. Arguments of this kind often result in conviction, without amounting to objective proof: one who has been convinced by them will not necessarily be able to communicate his satisfaction to another, and will certainly be quite unable to do so unless the other is willing to make his own imaginative effort and see the work in question in the way recommended. A personal element is involved here which recalls, even if it does not precisely reproduce, the feature which made Plato say that the final truths of his philosophy could not be written down.

But this is to anticipate. For the moment we need only insist that insight does enter into metaphysical thinking, and that its role should neither be forgotten nor exaggerated. It is forgotten, to take an extreme case, when opponents of metaphysics select random

1. See Chapter 11 below.

sentences from metaphysical treatises and criticize them as not immediately intelligible. It is exaggerated when reference to it is thought to be sufficient to cover total or virtual absence of argument, as happens when a Heraclitus or a Heidegger is put forward as the type of a metaphysical philosopher. There is perhaps a sense in which a metaphysical genius can claim to be a sage, in so far as he sees life steadily and sees it whole; it is also the case that the elaboration of a metaphysical vision often requires unusual conceptual subtlety. But neither of these circumstances excuses the pursuit of obscurity in metaphysics for its own sake; neither gives any warrant to the traditional caricature of the metaphysician as a man whom nobody understands but himself. To identify metaphysics with the oracular pronouncements of seers is no more justified than to equate it with a simple pursuit of knowledge of the occult.

6

The Limits of Reason: Descartes and
Cogito ergo sum

1. *Transcendent and immanent metaphysics*

WE HAVE now surveyed a number of metaphysical theories, and distinguished among them two main types, which can most conveniently be called by the old-fashioned terms 'transcendent' and 'immanent'. In systems such as Platonism the promise is held out that human reason, when properly put to work, can move beyond the confused and confusing world of sense to the unchanging realities which underlie it; this is at once a process of enlightenment and of liberation. By contrast materialists (and idealists too, if our interpretation of Hegel and Bradley is correct) show no disposition to turn their backs on everyday experience. For them the opposition between appearance and reality, central to all forms of metaphysical thinking, is between less and more adequate ways of taking what falls within experience. The possibility of transcending experience altogether is set aside as scarcely worth discussion.

It is already apparent that pure cases of transcendent and immanent metaphysical theories are hard to find. Plato and Plotinus are predominantly metaphysicians of the transcendent type, but the thought of Plato at least has a different side to it. Materialism as we have expounded it is a system whose whole concern is with the proper interpretation of experience, yet many of its opponents (Berkeley, for example) have condemned it on the ground that it involves an unjustifiable claim to knowledge of the supersensible. Add to this that other philosophies we have examined, such as that of Aristotle, belong unequivocally to neither type, and that there are many metaphysical systems which we have not so much as mentioned, and serious doubts will be thrown on the value of the whole classificatory scheme.

Despite this, I propose to take the scheme as affording an adequate, if somewhat rough, guide to a substantial amount of metaphysical literature, and to consider in the next three chapters what there is to be said for and against metaphysics on this basis.

The first point to notice here is that many of the standard criticisms of metaphysics are framed on the assumption that all metaphysics is transcendent. This is true in particular of the Kantian and Positivist criticisms outlined in Chapter 3. These critics took it as plain that metaphysicians are wanting to give us *information*, about the true nature of things or the world as a whole, and must thus set themselves up as rivals to empirical enquirers. Scientists on this account of the matter deal with appearances, metaphysicians with the reality which lies behind them; scientists produce contingent truths, metaphysicians (thanks to the superior nature of their subject-matter) truths which are both necessary and factual. The lines on which the critics in question treat this position have already been made plain. They hold, in effect, that there is an absolute gulf between truths of fact, which can be arrived at only on the basis of information provided by the senses, and truths of reason, which are either, as for the Positivists, purely verbal, mere tautologies, or, as for Kant, principles which serve to co-ordinate sense-experiences but lose all significance when applied outside the sphere of possible experience. The suggestion that reason could produce factual knowledge from its own unaided resources, or lay a valid claim to insight into the underlying essence of things, is accordingly discounted.

I have argued already that this attack loses its force when we turn from transcendent to immanent metaphysics, whose exponents cannot be properly charged with wanting to give information about anything, and who make no claim to knowledge of the supersensible. Whatever his faults, a metaphysician of this kind is certainly not a pseudo-scientist. I shall not revive these issues now, but shall take my previous conclusions for granted. Instead, I want to ask the unfashionable question whether Kant and the Positivists have really made their points against the alternative kind of metaphysics. Is it true that transcendent metaphysics has been shown to be impossible in principle?

2. *Reason as a primary source of knowledge*

A defender of transcendent metaphysics would, in my view, be under an obligation to meet the Kantian challenge set out on p. 40 above: he would have, that is to say, to make out either that intellectual intuition is a reality or that inferences from what is experienced to what lies outside experience are in certain circumstances legitimate. The first of these alternatives is perhaps not clear as it stands. I mean it to cover the suggestion that the intellect is a primary source of knowledge, just as the senses are primary sources of knowledge. Deprive a man of one of his senses, and you deprive him of an important range of cognitive data; a man who loses his sense of smell, for instance, is not in a position to pronounce on aspects of things which are accessible to other men. Suppose, *per impossibile*, it were possible for a man to keep his senses and be deprived of his intellect: would such a person lose access to a similar, though perhaps more important, range of truths? The question as it stands is plainly absurd, because we can clearly know nothing on the basis of sensing alone: intellectual operations are involved in the simplest judgment of sense. For our present purposes, however, we must set aside such operations, in which, to speak crudely, the initiative lies with the senses, and consider what the intellect might accomplish if it were disembodied and by itself. Would such a 'pure' intellect, to use the Platonic phrase, be in possession of *any* knowledge?

Aristotle glanced at this question in speaking of God, who was just such a pure intellect according to the argument of Book *Λ* of the *Metaphysics*; he said enigmatically that God's activity would consist in a (or the) 'knowing of knowing'. This pronouncement, if taken literally, is patently unsatisfactory, for God must first be engaged in cognitive activity before reflection on the operation could take place, and Aristotle does nothing to explain what *this* activity could be. The obvious suggestion that it might be first-hand knowing of the ordinary kind will not meet the case, seeing that such knowing, for Aristotle as for anyone else, is based on and develops out of sense-perception, and a pure intellect would have no senses, since it would, by definition, be unembodied. But if it is not ordinary first-hand knowing, what operation could it be?

A possible answer would be deductive reasoning of the mathematical kind; 'knowing of knowing' would then consist in second-order scrutiny of processes of demonstrative inference, and God would be condemned on this account to an eternity of formal logic. The objection might be made here that the ideas of mathematics, though remote from sense, are not literally innate: deprive a man of all his senses, and he will not be able to form an idea of *triangle*, or even of *one* and *two*. It seems, however, scarcely worth discussing the objection, since even if it could be met the theory would offer a very poor basis for transcendent metaphysics. Let it be allowed that logical ideas in a sense spring from the pure intellect: if they are its only products there will be no possibility whatever of establishing the nature of things by pure thought. A metaphysician can be equipped with as effective reasoning powers as you please; he will not be able to take a step towards his goal so long as this remains his sole equipment.

3. '*I exist*' *as a basic premise in metaphysics*

These conclusions might be accepted as formally correct by supporters of transcendent metaphysics; they would say, however, that the case for this sort of metaphysics is entirely misrepresented if we stop at this point. Aristotle's God, even if the situation about the 'knowing of knowing' were what we have asserted it to be, need not confine himself to the sphere of formal logic. For there is at least one material proposition which such a being would be in a position to affirm, namely that he existed. Affirmation of one's own existence is not bound up, on this view of the matter, with the possession of senses; a being whose whole nature was intellectual would be as well entitled to make it as a man. But once this point is granted the way to metaphysical construction lies open. Given what is sometimes called the primary intuition of being involved in the undeniable fact of one's own existence, it will be possible to infer the essential nature of reality as such.

The issue which must be faced here is whether affirmation of one's own existence amounts to what I have just grandiloquently called a 'primary intuition of being'; a less pretentious way of putting it would be to ask if it involved the assertion of a genuine truth of fact. As the preceding argument has shown, a metaphysician needs at least one such truth if he is to claim any solid basis for his system, and if he is a transcendent metaphysician, who puts his trust in the intellect as opposed to the senses, he will need to show that the truth in question is intellectually impregnable. Now the proposition that *I am* or *exist* seems to fulfil both requirements. It states what seems to be a truth about the world and is nevertheless such that its denial seems to run one into absurdity: in attempting to deny that I exist I reaffirm that I exist. But the position is perhaps not so clear as Descartes and others who have followed this line of argument have supposed.

Is it obvious in the first place that I state a truth of fact if I say that I exist? The first difficulty about the question is to know how to take it. The fact is, of course, as modern linguistic philosophers have pointed out, that people very rarely say anything so extraordinary as that they exist. One real context in which something like this form of words could be used would be if a man were persistently ignored by his companions generally or by one particular person; he might then break out with the words 'I exist too' or say 'She treats me as if I just didn't exist'. It seems clear that in the circumstances envisaged existence has got something to do with importance: to say one exists is, in a way, to say one deserves attention (and of course to imply that one is not getting it). But if this is correct affirming existence comes down to staking a claim rather than stating a fact, and no primary intuition of being is involved in an utterance of that sort.

It might be argued that a man who said 'She treats me as if I just didn't exist' would mean to assert a fact as well as to stake a claim, the fact namely that he formed part of the real order of things and was not merely fictitious. If this could be extended to the case of 'I exist too' the metaphysician's requirements would seem to be satisfied. And they certainly would be in so far as he would now have at his disposal a genuine, if somewhat unusual, truth of fact. The trouble is that *this* truth does not seem to be intellectually impregnable, as can be seen if we spell it out in more detail. To say I exist in the sense required is to say that my activities have effects on and are affected by what goes on in the real world of things in space and time; I am not an impotent ghost or idle figment of the imagination, but an actual existent whose presence cannot be safely ignored. Now can all this be got out of the seemingly innocent words 'I exist'? The fact that the words are uttered at all shows that something is real; the fact that I utter them shows me that I am real. But what 'real' means in each case is something which has to be established on the basis of experience; the criteria for its application are not implicit in the bare proposition 'I exist'. If I were Aristotle's God, who was totally unconcerned with the rest of the universe and entirely unaffected by it, they would presumably be quite different from what they are for a human being.

Empiricist philosophers since Hume and Kant have repeatedly said that existence is not a genuine predicate. I do not myself believe that this is correct for all uses of the term 'exist', or there would be no sense in saying things like 'I simply don't exist as far as she is concerned'. I am prepared again to allow that it is significant to ascribe existence to concrete things like cats and at the same time to deny it to abstractions such as charity. But I think even so that there is enough truth in the empiricist doctrine to undermine the metaphysical case we are discussing. The point can be put by saying that, if we do distinguish instances in which existence is a genuine predicate from others where it is not, it is with cases of the latter kind that the metaphysicians in question have been concerned. Descartes thought that 'I am' followed from 'I think', though not apparently from 'I walk'. The truth is that it follows from any phrase in which the word 'I' appears, for it is the pronoun which carries the commitment to existence rather than the content of what is said. The same is true of course of any demonstrative or individuating expression: it would make nonsense to use such words except with the implication that they apply to something, and therefore that that something exists. But nothing can be inferred from this fact, as applied to a particular case, either about the character of the something in question or about the kind of existence it enjoys. As Professor Ayer put it,[1] the 'I exist' which is implicit in 'I think' is a degenerate proposition, in the sense that the predicate adds nothing to what we are already committed to by the use of the subject-term. An utterance of this sort, if not literally tautological, is so near to being a tautology as to be entirely useless as a basis for metaphysical construction.

4. Descartes' exploitation of the cogito argument

Yet the fact remains that many metaphysicians have thought they could build something significant on the proposition that *I exist*, or on its more general counterpart *something exists*. Descartes, for example, thought that he could assert on the strength of the *cogito* argument (a) that his mind was distinct from his body; (b) that what he really was was a substance whose whole nature consisted in thought; and (c) that despite this description he was not truly self-dependent, but owed his existence to something outside him, which turned out in the end to be the 'necessary' being God. Here we have the 'primary intuition of being' with a vengeance: the whole weight of the Cartesian system is contained in these simple premises. It may be instructive to enquire on what basis Descartes thought he could set them up.

Two sets of arguments used by Descartes are important in this connection. First, the sceptical considerations adduced at the beginning of the *Meditations* with the object of showing that our everyday convictions about the existence of material things are less well founded than we think. The conclusion which these purport to establish is that we can never be sure of the truth of a statement such as *I see an orange* (since the possibility that we might be dreaming cannot be definitively ruled out), though we can be sure of the truth of some other proposition on each such occasion, in the case given the proposition that *I seem to see an orange* or *I have the experience of seeing an orange*. These latter propositions are alleged to be true whether or not there is an actual orange to be seen; they are true if the orange exists only in my dream. Now these propositions are, broadly, concerned with our mental experiences, and

1. In *The Problem of Knowledge*, Penguin Books (1956).

it is claimed accordingly that minds, or mental experiences, are 'more easily known' than bodies. It is concluded further that the word 'I' strictly refers only to mind or mental experiences, since these are the only things about whose existence or occurrence I can be absolutely sure.

Is it true that all statements about material things or happenings in the physical world are open to doubt, whereas corresponding statements about mental experiences are not? Descartes employed two arguments in support of this conclusion, the argument from illusion and the argument from dreaming. The argument from illusion begins with the assertion that there are occasions on which we are clearly mistaken in our perceptual judgments and goes on to maintain that there is no intrinsic difference, at the time of their occurrence, between the perceptual experiences we take to be veridical and those we subsequently reject as illusory; the conclusion is that we *may* be mistaken in *all* our perceptual judgments. The argument from dreaming proceeds on precisely the same lines, except that the initial premise is that we sometimes take objects to exist in reality when they exist only in our dreams and the conclusion that we may be dreaming all the time.

Now there seems to be a fundamental incoherence in any argument of this sort, springing from the fact that if the conclusion is true the premises cannot be set up. Suppose that it were indeed the case that not one of our perceptual experiences could be warranted as reliable: we should never be in a position to say that we are sometimes deceived in our sense-judgments, for in the circumstances envisaged we should not know what it was not to be so deceived. In order to decide that we were mistaken on a particular occasion we need to be able to contrast the experiences we had then with others which we take to be non-deceptive; if no sense-experience can be taken as being in order the contrast cannot be made. Similarly with dreaming. Were it really the case that, as Descartes put it, 'there exist no certain marks' by which to distinguish waking from dreaming, we could never formulate the premise that we sometimes think we are perceiving things when all the time we are dreaming. It would not be possible to say, as Descartes wants to say, things like 'I thought I was awake and sitting in my room, but it subsequently turned out that I was dreaming'.

There are many other difficulties in Descartes' position, but the above remarks should suffice to show that his grounds for maintaining that the only thing of whose existence I can be initially sure is my own existence as a mind were quite inadequate. So far is this from being true, indeed, that I could not assert that I existed unless I knew that something else existed as well: I should not have the requisite idea of myself. It follows that one part at least of the construction which Descartes put on the basic proposition of his metaphysics—the supposedly undeniable premise that *I exist*— was mistaken. Deprive Descartes of his arguments for scepticism about the senses, and he will not be able to give any plausibility to the proposition that he is a substance whose essence consists in thinking. It remains to be seen whether his other contention, that he knows himself to be a being dependent for its existence on something outside itself, is any better supported.

5. Descartes and contingent being

The main ground on which Descartes relies here is that he knows himself to be an imperfect being and that such a being cannot be truly self-contained. That he is an imperfect being is taken to be so obvious as scarcely to need arguing; if argument were called for it would be enough to mention such things as that human knowledge is limited both in extent and arrangement (there are many things in the universe that I do not understand, and in any case I cannot understand everything at once) and that the human will, though formally unlimited (there is nothing in the world I could not wish for), is in practice limited in all sorts of ways: people most certainly cannot do whatever they want.

These deficiencies are taken by Descartes as evidence that he is not self-sufficient, and therefore 'not alone in the world', in the following way. First, it is argued that were he truly self-sufficient he must also be self-creating, and would not have created himself less than perfect, i.e. with the limitations referred to. Secondly and more interestingly, the suggestion is made that the very fact that he recognizes his imperfections argues that he must be in possession of a positive idea of perfection, an idea he could not have derived from himself.

I do not wish to discuss here Descartes' contention that God is the only possible source from which he could have got the idea of perfection; my immediate concern is with the less ambitious thesis that he could not himself have originated the idea. A decision on this perhaps not wholly perspicuous issue turns on what we take the idea to comprise. As already mentioned, Descartes took it to be a positive idea, which is to say that he was not prepared to define it in terms of his own capacities raised to an indefinitely higher degree: the perfect being, he insisted, has infinite capacities, and there is all the difference in the world between such capacities and those just described. The trouble with this is to know how Descartes can justify his assertion. To do so he would have to explain what he meant by e.g. perfect knowledge without *merely* saying that it is knowledge like the human, but with the limitations of human knowledge removed. I confess that I cannot see what he could say over and above this. But if he were forced to concede that his idea of the perfect is really to be understood in a negative way, his thesis that we owe it to something outside ourselves is very much less plausible.

It may be said that all Descartes needs to be assured of the truth of his view that he is not self-dependent is the admission that he has the ability to handle the concepts of *better* and *worse*. To talk of better and worse presupposes reference to a standard, and we cannot simultaneously hold that we are less than we should like to be and find the standard in ourselves. Plato put forward a version of this argument in the *Phaedo*, and it cannot be denied that it has an immediate popular appeal. It owes some of its plausibility, however, to the mistaken view that there are no standards other than absolute standards, things which are scarcely to be found in this imperfect world. The truth is rather that we can take all sorts of things, real and imaginary, as standards by which to judge in particular cases, including, exceptionally, what we have ourselves done in the past. I may well judge that my present conduct leaves something to be desired because it falls short of some earlier action of mine which I now view with complete approval. To be self-satisfied to this degree is perhaps rash, but involves no logical absurdity. But it would be a mistake in any case to think that I can only operate with an ideal if I am acquainted with some object from which the ideal is copied. I do not need to have met the Perfect Cricketer in order to judge that some people are better cricketers than others.

The import of these remarks should not be misunderstood. I have not meant to deny the obvious empirical truth that human beings do not bring themselves into existence but are dependent in this respect on their parents, nor the plain fact that in assessing behaviour they tend to take other people as their standards. But it is not with mundane facts of this sort that Descartes and his fellow metaphysicians are concerned, as Descartes himself makes clear over the matter of his dependence on his parents. The proposition they seek to establish is that there exists something which is *of its nature* contingent; given the truth of this they can proceed to establish not mere empirical dependencies but the necessity for affirming the existence of something which is outside the empirical sphere altogether and exists necessarily or through its own nature. The object of the preceding discussion has been to show that Descartes offers no good grounds for advancing from *I exist*, which is in a sense indubitable, to *I exist as a contingent being*, which he needs as a starting-point for his version of the First Cause argument. He purports to ground his metaphysics on a basis which is intellectually unchallengeable, but it turns out to be nothing of the sort.

6. *Further remarks on Cartesianism*

A defender of Descartes might reply that it is a mistake to treat Cartesian metaphysics as a strictly intellectual system: it rests indeed on a primary intuition, an intuition of the self as a limited being. What we have to do with here might be called an immediate insight into fact, rather than a proposition which is logically compulsive. On this I would make two comments. First, that whatever the truth about Descartes' own attitude to his basic propositions, there can be no doubt that he wishes to give the impression that his metaphysical system *is* logically compulsive. The contrast he draws between common-sense beliefs which, however seemingly well authenticated, are open to sceptical doubts unanswerable at the theoretical level, and the propositions *I exist* and *God exists*, which are at least as certain as any truth in mathematics, is one piece of evidence in favour of this statement; another is the special stress he lays on the *cogito* argument, which issues in a truth that it is seemingly impossible to deny. Some later metaphysicians, such as Bradley, have said that metaphysics ought to rest on propositions which are such that their truth is involved in their own attempted denial; there can be little doubt that they were taking Descartes as their model here. It may be of course that their promise here was not matched by their performance—in Bradley's own case I believe that this is certainly true—but this does not alter what they thought they were doing.

To take Descartes as a metaphysician who sought to determine the nature of things by purely conceptual considerations, which is in fact what we have been doing, is accordingly quite legitimate. And if it is said that this is to stress the letter of the Cartesian philosophy at the expense of its spirit, I should agree that this could indeed be true, but would point out secondly that the alternative course of grounding it on one or more 'basic intuitions' is not without its difficulties. The trouble with intuitions of any sort is that they lay claim to self-evidence, but cannot be proved. Nor could it be said that the predicament of the metaphysician here is exactly that of the common man, since there are many things which the latter is prepared to affirm but could not prove, e.g. *this is blue*. The difference is that such propositions are widely accepted and acted on, whereas their alleged metaphysical counterparts command no comparable general assent, even among professing metaphysicians. What seems clear and obvious to one will be highly disputable, or even plainly false, to another.

At the end of the previous chapter (pp. 81 ff.) I pointed out that there is a sense in which every system of immanent metaphysics may be said to rest on a certain vision or intuition of the world as a whole, and I must make clear that what has just been said is not intended to amend or invalidate the view there expressed. Why then is intuition supposed to be respectable when indulged in by a Bradley or a Hegel, but not when appealed to by a Descartes? If there is a satisfactory answer to this question, it must be found in the types of things which the different philosophers concerned claim to intuit.

The imaginative insight on which, say, Bradley built his meta-physics is on any account highly general: it is a vision of reality as a single self-differentiating whole, a true unity in diversity. A vision of this kind does not provide a premise on which the metaphysician subsequently builds; its function is rather to suggest an interpreta-tive scheme, which has to be elaborated and defended by further argument. For this reason there is a sense in which it can be checked: the value of an intuition of this kind lies in its suggestive power, and if this proves disappointing (if it turns out that the interpretative scheme recommended can be applied only if a blind eye is turned on a number of obvious facts or features of experience) it can scarcely be expected to maintain its appeal. An intuition of this kind might thus be said to spread beyond itself, and to give hostages to fortune just because of that fact. By contrast the basic intuition of the self as a limited and contingent being which some commentators attribute to Descartes is self-contained and because of that uncheckable: given its truth all sorts of things are supposed to follow, but whether or not they do is not itself a test of its authenticity. The reason for this, put shortly, is that the alleged intuition is here supposed to provide a premise, not a presupposition. If metaphysicians are to be allowed to validate the basic premises of their systems by appeal to intuition their task becomes altogether too easy.

It should perhaps be added that the above criticisms of Descartes have been directed against what may be called the formal articula-tion of the Cartesian system. On the face of it Descartes sets out from a truth which is at once necessary and factual and professes to proceed, by a series of steps which are logically necessary, to con-clusions about God, who is certainly not a possible object of human experience as here conceived. He thus appears to be a transcendent metaphysician *par excellence*, and it is from this point of view that his ideas have been considered in this chapter. But it is by no means impossible to look at these ideas in quite a different way, and to see them as the attempted resolution of a somewhat less formal and abstract problem. This was the problem of how to do justice to the full possibilities of mechanical science of nature without overthrow-ing the traditional Christian picture of man as a being at once natural and supernatural. The rise of physics, which had begun in the generation before Descartes' own, threatened to carry with it the triumph of a philosophy of materialism; and Descartes, who had unbounded confidence in the prospects of the new science, was acutely aware of this threat. He sought to meet it by a division of spheres of influence: body, including the human body, could be handed over to the physicists and understood in exclusively mechanical terms, whilst mind was reserved for theologians and philosophers and taken to be a different sort of thing altogether. In offering this compromise, which has still not entirely lost its appeal, Descartes was proposing what he took to be a reasoned alternative to materialism, a new comprehensive philosophy which could take the place of the scholasticism to which the Christian Church had previously pinned its faith. It was an essential part of this philosophy, as it had been of Aristotle's, that there exist things, namely God and human souls, which cannot be known in sense-experience. But this fact no more precludes our taking the whole system as offering an overall interpretation of experience in the one case than it does in the other.

7

The Limits of Reason: Hume and Causality

1. *Inference from the sensible to the supersensible*

MY OBJECT in the preceding chapter has been to re-examine the
case for saying that the human mind is a primary source of knowledge, in the sense explained on p. 86 above. But it is only fair to point
out that there are many supporters of transcendent metaphysics,
in particular all those who draw their inspiration from Thomas
Aquinas, who would regard that view as extravagant and indeed
quite indefensible. That 'there is nothing in the intellect which was
not previously in the senses' seems to them axiomatic: the metaphysician, like any other enquirer, has no choice but to start from
empirical premises. But though he must begin from experience, it
does not follow that his thinking has to remain within the bounds of
the experienceable. He can proceed from what is given in sense-
experience to the intelligible reality which lies behind it thanks to
his possession of certain rational principles, such as the principles of
substance and causality.

It was against this estimate of the possibilities of knowledge of the
supersensible that Hume and Kant directed their main attacks. Of
the two Hume was very much the brusquer. The scholastic philosophy with its talk of substance and accident was in his opinion mere
play with words, the very notion of substance being 'an unintelligible
chimera' when not taken as the collective name of a set of empirical
properties. Causality was a different matter, since it was only by
causal arguments that we could proceed beyond what was immediately given in experience. But Hume insisted in the first place

that it was a gross error to suppose that any such argument could take us beyond experience altogether: on its objective side the causal relation was nothing but a relation of regular precedence and succession in time, so that only what fell within time could be causally connected. And secondly he argued that there was no warrant for supposing that causal inference was an operation of the understanding strictly so called. We moved from effect to cause or cause to effect not because we had insight into any real connection between the two (all events were loose and separate, and therefore there were only external links between them), but because we were determined by nature or custom so to do. Causality was strictly not an intelligible relation.

2. *Hume on causality*

Since anyone who wants to maintain that transcendent metaphysics is a real possibility has got to come to terms with Hume, I shall proceed now to ask what, if anything, is wrong with his account of causality.

Let me first elaborate his view a little further. We all think initially that a cause produces or brings about its effect, and we think we can see in particular cases how and why it does so. Hume is anxious in the first place to show that the connection involved is not a logical connection, like that between the premises of a deductive argument and its conclusion; if it were we should be able to say in advance of experience what would cause what, whereas it is only in experience that we learn that fire burns and water suffocates. There is an intrinsic connection—if you like, a connection of meaning—between premises and conclusion in the case given; by contrast the connection between a cause and its effect is always external, there being nothing in the nature of the one which of itself points forward to the other. It follows that, in principle, anything can cause anything: any two events can be linked together by this particular relationship.

In practice, however, we find that the relationship is somewhat more restricted. For us to say that one thing is the cause of another it must be true (a) that the first preceded the second in time, and (b) that things of the first kind have been observed to precede things of the second kind regularly. Given these conditions, we form a habit of expecting the second when the first is presented; we feel an impulse to pass from the impression of the one to the idea of the other. And Hume says that it is this fact which explains our conviction that causes necessitate their effects; the necessity lies not in the objective facts, but in the mind of the observer. As for the alleged insight into the connection claimed for particular cases, that is simply an illusion provoked by familiarity. Because we have long experience of certain kinds of causal connection we think we can see why they hold as they do. But if we look at the facts carefully we see that no such claim could be justified.

This analysis of causality in terms of regular succession plus subjective necessity has met with sharp criticism. It is said in the first place to cover far too much. Thus it fails to differentiate between the causal relation proper and the analogous but nevertheless quite distinct relation of sign and thing signified. That the cows sit down in certain conditions may be a sign of rain, but is certainly not its cause. Yet Hume's requirements could be satisfied in this case quite as well as in one of genuine causal connection: cows sitting down in the conditions in question might always have been followed by wet weather, and an observer could feel a strong impulse to pass from the impression of the one to the thought of the other. It would seem from this that Hume at best enumerated *some* of the requirements which have to be fulfilled if one thing is to be said to be the cause of another. A further difficulty of a similar kind is found if we reflect that, on Hume's account of the matter, any regular antecedent of a phenomenon would have to be denominated a cause, or part-cause, of the phenomenon. In practice, however, we draw a distinction between the factor in the situation which we reckon to be *the* cause and a whole lot of other factors which are, perhaps, regular constituents of situations of this sort but are nevertheless set aside as mere conditions of its outcome. Hume does nothing to help us make this distinction either.

3. *Cause as a practical notion*

These criticisms are fully justified, but they can be met without any fundamental alteration in Hume's position. To meet them we have only to pay attention to an aspect of causality on which recent philosophers have properly insisted but about which Hume is unfortunately silent: the fact that the search for causes is often (and perhaps primarily) a practical matter.[1] In looking for the cause of something (the cause of a disease, for instance, or of a certain kind of social phenomenon) we are often trying to put our fingers on a factor in the antecedent situation the control of which will enable us to bring about or avert the phenomenon in question. Causing is here closely associated with action, so much so that to say that we do not know the cause of something or other is to say that we do not know what to do to produce or prevent it.

The differences between signs and causes becomes immediately clear on this account: if A is a sign of B, removing A will not prevent B occurring, as it will if A is the cause of B. To illustrate: if the fact that the cows sit down is only a sign that rain will come, keeping them on their feet will not ensure dry weather.

The difference between causes and conditions is perhaps not so simple, though again it has something to do with the distinction between the factors in the situation over which we can and those over which we cannot exercise control. That I should be breathing is no doubt a condition of my catching smallpox, but if I did get the disease the fact that I was breathing would scarcely be said to be responsible. One reason for describing contact with a smallpox victim as the cause of my being infected and breathing as a mere condition is that the first could, given suitable knowledge and care, have been prevented, whereas for practical purposes the second could not. But there is more to it than this. As Collingwood pointed out, the picking out of causes in practical situations depends not only on what factors can be controlled but also on the interests and functions of the parties concerned. An honest member of the highways department will ascribe an accident to the state of the road surface and dismiss the fact that the tyres of the car which went into a skid did not grip as well as expected; an honest car manufacturer may well reverse the roles. Both factors are here eliminable and therefore both qualify as causes, but it is not the business of either party to

1. Cf. e.g. R. G. Collingwood, *An Essay on Metaphysics* (Oxford, 1940), pp. 296 ff.; D. T. Gasking, 'Causation and Recipes', *Mind* (1955).

eliminate both, and each regards what does not fall within his province as condition rather than cause.

It should be emphasized that knowledge of causes in this practical sense requires no theoretical understanding of the connection between cause and effect: provided I know how to produce or prevent the effect, however the knowledge has been acquired, I may be said to know the cause. It was because of this absence of theoretical commitment that I said above that Hume could incorporate this aspect of causality into his analysis without fundamentally altering it. Hume wishes to discredit the commonly accepted view that there is an essential connection between finding causes and gaining an insight into the structure of fact. The philosophers who stress the practical side of causality have no such general axe to grind, but the effect of their work, at least as we have so far taken it, is to reinforce Hume's conclusion. Yet it could well be argued that this conclusion, whether in Hume's version or in that of his modern successors, is frankly incredible. The search for causes may begin as a practical matter and be sustained by a practical impetus, but to take it as exclusively practical seems quite absurd. For after all even in the most pedestrian contexts we bring theory to bear in our causal diagnosis; we pick out a certain factor as the cause not because we have discovered its efficacy by trial and error like a child, but because we know on general theoretical grounds what effect it is likely to have. In other words, the discovery of causes goes hand in hand not just with prevention or production, still less with mere prediction, but also with the giving of explanations. Hume's account of this side of the matter is at first sight far from plausible.

4. *Causal terminology as 'theory-loaded'*

Since the point at issue in this discussion is the rationality of the concept of causation it may be useful at this juncture to look at a modern view which is directly opposed to Hume's and then consider why Hume would reject it. The view is that causal terminology is, in a phrase of Professor Ryle's, all 'theory-loaded'.[1] Hume speaks as if causal transactions always took place between events which

1. Cf. N. R. Hanson, 'Causal Chains', *Mind* (1955).

were described in entire independence of one another; this is why, for him, anything can cause anything. But if we look at actual causal language, particularly as we find it in technical contexts, we see that it is not neutral in the Humean way. A doctor, inspecting an irregularity on a man's face, sees it as a scar and thinks that it must have been caused by a severe wound. Both 'wound' and 'scar' are technical terms here, and what is more they are interdefinable. When the doctor decided that the irregularity was a scar, he was already committed to saying it had been caused by a wound. Nor is a wound something that can be followed by anything you please: on the contrary, it is what gives rise to a scar. An element of theory may be said to be built into the very description which the doctor gives, though admittedly it is not in this case very advanced theory. And the same is true of many descriptions, whether their language is technical (as when a mechanic tells me that the trouble with my car is a fault in the fuel pump) or simply that of sophisticated everyday life (as when a social commentator remarks that a revolutionary situation is building up). In all such cases we commit ourselves, in the act of describing what is before us, to a judgment about what is going to happen: our words, if appropriate (and this is of course the all-important condition), bind the future as well as characterize the present. And in these circumstances we are concerned not with events which are loose and separate like Hume's, but with facts which are intimately linked with other facts, with events which point backward to what happened in the past and forward to what is due to happen in the future.

If we ask now why Hume could not accept such an account, the answer will be found in what he has to say about the immediate objects of knowledge. The only things of whose existence we can be certain were, he thought, either immediately presented impressions or their fainter copies, ideas. And the only descriptions which can be accepted as wholly authentic are such as confine themselves to these immediate objects, without any precarious commitment to the future or doubtful reference to the past. Descriptions of this sort must be given in terms which carry no theoretical load, such as 'sweet', 'loud' and 'pungent'. Hume would not have denied that we commonly make use of a different way of speaking which was far less guarded; what he wanted to know was what justified us in so doing. His own view was that there could be no rational justification. Distinct and continuing 'objects', as opposed to 'impressions', were fictions of the imagination, foisted on us by custom or habit; we could not help thinking in terms of them, but this did not make it appropriate to conclude that we have any real insight into connections of fact. There was not and indeed could not be any such insight, for the only real facts were facts about things which were in their very nature unrelated.

Nor would Hume have been impressed by the argument that the cases in which the reverse seems to be most obviously true are to be met with in scientific contexts. 'The most perfect philosophy of the natural kind', he said in a typical passage in the *Enquiry*, 'only staves off our ignorance a little':[1] we must not think that bringing a phenomenon under scientific laws enables us to understand it in any real sense. Such laws may make it possible to predict, given the ultimate assumption that the future will be conformable to the past, but they can scarcely claim to explain. 'Ultimate' causes and the 'secret springs' which lie behind what happens in the natural world are past finding out. Science is, at bottom, a series of merely juxtaposed generalities, or again a set of rules, with no real internal connections, for manipulating the world. If it has an importance, it is practical, not theoretical.

5. *Criticism of Hume's assumptions*

One might very well object that this picture of science bears little resemblance to what goes on in advanced sciences today: the element of theory, on which Plato was already insisting (see pp. 29–30 above), is now recognized as all-important, yet Hume appears to ignore it altogether. But to refute Hume decisively we must overthrow his positive conviction that the only true descriptions are those which are given in neutral, non-theoretical terms. This view, as we saw, was bound up with his account of impressions and ideas as the sole immediate objects of knowledge, which account in its turn was determined by his acceptance of the sceptical arguments about common-sense perceptual beliefs advanced by Descartes

1. *Enquiry concerning Human Understanding* (ed. Selby-Bigge), p. 31.

(Hume produced variations on these arguments,[1] but his position about them was in essence Cartesian). If we dismiss these, on the grounds advanced in the previous chapter, the myth of impressions as the only solid facts can be dissolved, and we can feel quite sure that we are sometimes directly aware of things, not just of impressions in our minds. It follows that the terminology of material objects, which as Hume rightly saw takes us beyond the here and now, is sometimes correctly used. But if it is also true that causal connections are built into that terminology, in the way sketched above, we can feel confident that such connections are part and parcel of the structure of fact. So far from its being true, as Hume pretends, that reality consists of loose and separate events following one another in regular ways and becoming 'associated' in our minds thanks to their constant conjunction, we have to acknowledge that events are intimately connected one with another in virtue of the very descriptions we give of them. If it is true that X has a scar on his face now, it must also be true that at some time in the past he suffered what is called in medical circles a wound. You cannot have the one fact without the other. And statements which purport to assert facts of this kind cannot all be set aside as open to doubt, as Hume mistakenly supposed.

I conclude from this that Hume's attempt to demonstrate that causal reasoning is not an act of the understanding is as untenable as it is paradoxical. For a great many purposes description and explanation go hand in hand, and the more sophisticated we are the larger the element of theory which enters into our characterization of reality. Not that what was said above about the practical aspect of causality is unimportant. The enquiry into causes is often, and perhaps typically, a practical enquiry. And it could be, if necessary, an exclusively practical undertaking: beings with no grasp of theory could nevertheless learn what caused what by simple trial and error, as rats and monkeys perhaps do. But it would be idle to pretend that civilized human beings are in this state, even if savages approximate to it. There are few occasions where we lack all theoretical understanding of the situations we confront; practical causal diagnosis is normally carried out against a background of partial knowledge at least. We should none of us feel very happy with a

1. In the *Treatise* I, iv, 2.

doctor who disclaimed all knowledge of the workings of the body
and put his trust exclusively in the sort of know-how old wives are
alleged to have. Yet according to Hume no one can do better than
that.

6. *Causality and metaphysics*

The conclusion that causality is, as transcendent metaphysicians
claim, a rational concept follows inevitably: there are no such things
as events without causes. But though it is true that every fact as it
were points outwards to other facts, this is not enough in itself to
justify the transcendent metaphysician's inference that the whole
system of facts is such that we need to postulate something outside
it to make it intelligible at all. The web of facts, or of events if that
term is preferred, may be said to radiate outwards from what each of
us takes to be the case now. Our judgment about what exists in the
present commits us to further judgments both about what once
existed and about what will exist, and these in turn carry a commitment to other judgments of the same general kind. The process is
indefinitely extensible—whatever existent we acknowledge we must
always go on to some other—but there seems to be nothing fundamentally incoherent in that. Nor is it the case that at any stage in
the process we pass outside the range of the experienceable. The
things whose existence we find ourselves forced to accept as bound
up with what is immediately before us have the same general characteristics as the latter: if the immediate objects of our knowledge exist
in space and time, so must the remoter. To that extent Hume was
correct, despite his imperfect account of the causal relation. For
though we have argued that the very description we give of some
events commits us to the judgment that other events have occurred,
the connections here in question are one and all connections between
events, i.e. happenings of the sort with which we are familiar. Even
if we defined the causal relation as a relation which is intelligible in
terms of a theory (a definition which would be appropriate to the
scientific cases at least), the *relata* have still got to be of the same
general kind.

One of Hume's main arguments in favour of the opaque character of causal relations was that we have to wait on experience to find out what will cause what; we cannot discern the causal properties of things *a priori*. It is important to stress that this argument retains its main force even if the above criticisms of Hume are accepted. Certainly we must now say that prediction of the outcome of a situation is involved in the way we describe it, particularly when the description is technical. But in the first place the theory which underlies such a description will itself contain propositions whose truth must either be presumed or accepted on the evidence of experience alone: the best of theories cannot claim to deduce all the propositions of which it consists. And secondly, whatever description we give of the situation, whilst it is true that it will always be legitimate to enquire why it took that particular form, the process of explanation is in the nature of things one that can never be complete. However far we carry it, we must always end in a position where we say: 'That is how things are, whatever the explanation.' In other words, every causal explanation involves some propositions which, for all our efforts to find intelligibility in the world, remain truly contingent. The truth about causal necessity is no doubt very different from what Hume thought: not all facts are, as he implied, equally 'brute', even though it is true that the opposite of any statement about matter of fact and existence is conceivable. But that there are brute facts, truths about the world which we just have to accept, would seem undeniable.

Some recent philosophers, sympathetic to the old metaphysical tradition, have said that there is a problem about why anything should exist at all. To ask why anything should exist at all is to refuse to accept that there are any brute facts. The same attitude was taken up by the seventeenth-century Rationalists, and in a different way by the Idealists two centuries later, when they argued that the existence of contingent things itself required the existence of something which existed necessarily. There must be a final reason for things being what they are. But the difficulty is to see what form that reason could take. The older metaphysicians found a solution to the problem by postulating a being which lay outside the sphere of the contingent altogether and was *causa sui*. Their modern counterparts talk in terms of facts, not of existents. Yet what sort of fact could possibly be such that it did not point beyond itself? Suppose that we answered the question 'Why should anything exist at all?' by saying that God chose that it should: in what way could that be a satisfying or a final answer? Only if we remove God from the sphere of existence will a reference to God's choice give anything like a final reason. But we can only do that, as the metaphysicians did, by an act which is essentially arbitrary. Far better to realize that the question about a first cause or ultimate reason for anything existing is ill posed. The simple truth is that in the nature of things we cannot explain everything. And this is a matter of logic, not of how the world is.

7. Concluding comment

It has been possible in this chapter and the last to discuss only a few of the standard arguments used by metaphysicians who profess to deduce the nature of things from purely intellectual considerations, or to penetrate from things sensible to things intelligible with the aid of rational principles. My main reason for not attempting a more general treatment is that such a treatment is available for anyone who wants it—in the 850 pages of the *Critique of Pure Reason*. The arguments there advanced seem to me definitive; I certainly know of no attempt to answer them which is in the least convincing. But a discussion such as Kant's obtains its generality only at the cost of a certain element of abstraction: although Kant clearly has particular metaphysical moves in mind throughout his book, he tends to state these in his own peculiar terminology and to leave the reader to make the connection with what actual metaphysicians have said. Kant's readers in 1781 were perhaps better equipped for this purpose than are his readers today. It seemed to me in these circumstances that a more piecemeal approach, in which an effort was made to examine one or two specific arguments which have something of an immediate appeal, would at least have supplementary value.

Has it been shown that transcendent metaphysics is impossible? Clearly not in the present discussion, in so far as there is much else to say on the subject (there is, for instance, the whole question of whether a metaphysical use can be made of the concept of substance, on which Hume is, to say the least, hasty). The most that could be claimed on the strength of the above arguments is that certain commonly attempted inferences cannot be made. And it is only fair to remark that even on these points there has been no demonstration that talk about the supersensible is nonsensical. In discussing causality we emphasized the theoretical background presupposed in much of our actual causal diagnosis, and argued that a Humean analysis of the causal relation was no longer tenable when this feature was taken into account. But if we look at scientific theories, classical or contemporary, we see that they regularly make reference to entities which are not to be met with in experience; the fundamental particles of modern physics are striking examples of such entities. To postulate the existence of what are in effect supersensible realities is held by the scientist to be necessary if he is, in the Platonic phrase, to 'save the phenomena'; sufficient warrant for believing in them can be found in the given empirical facts. And it may well be asked why, if this line of argument is admissible for the scientist, it should not also be open to the metaphysician. If the existence of electrons or mesons can be made intelligible by reference to empirical data, why cannot that of monads or Forms?

One possible answer to this is that there are clearer empirical criteria for deciding whether one is right or wrong in postulating mesons than for making the parallel decision about monads: it is known more clearly what talk about mesons leads one to expect, and there are therefore specifiable situations whose occurrence would tend to legitimize such talk and whose non-occurrence would tend to make it dubious. A philosopher like Leibniz, by contrast, can point to phenomena which tend to support his hypothesis (as in fact he does in the *Monadology*), but is less good at indicating what would have to be true for us to decide that it was false. It does not, however, follow from this that the distinction between science and metaphysics is here absolute; the old charge that a metaphysical theory is compatible with the occurrence of any facts whatsoever remains at this stage no more than an unjustified slur. But further discussion of the issue must be postponed till we take up the whole question of the validation of metaphysical statements, and meantime we must notice that until it is dealt with the case against transcendent metaphysics is formally incomplete.

8

Contemporary Anti-metaphysics

1. *Appearance and reality*

IN THE sketch of the philosophy of Plato with which this book began
the point of departure was Plato's sharp and all-important contrast
between knowledge and belief. Plain men and Sophists, for all the
latter's pretensions to insight, pass their lives in the confused state
of belief: their true understanding of themselves and of the world
about them is nil. Philosophers alone are acquainted with reality
and consequently they alone can appreciate the extent to which non-
philosophers are deceived in their estimate of the situation. In support of his claims here Plato proffered not only positive arguments
in favour of Forms as the only realities, but also destructive criticism
of what a later generation was to identify as the cause of common
sense. He held, for instance, as we have already made clear, that
knowledge through the senses is impossible in principle, for the
reason that objects of knowledge must really have the qualities they
seem to have, a requirement which the constantly changing objects
of sense-experience are unable to fulfil. Now it seems clear that anyone who is going to take Plato's account of 'reality' with any seriousness must first be prepared to accept what he has to say about
'appearances'; he must, that is, be ready to follow Plato in finding
serious difficulties in accepting anything like a common-sense view
of the world. Conversely, someone who thinks there is nothing
wrong in principle with everyday claims to knowledge of the kind we
associate with common sense will have a strong disposition to reject
Plato's whole metaphysics as founded on a mistake.

The position we have described is not peculiar to Plato, nor for
that matter to metaphysicians of the transcendent type. On the

contrary, it is typical of metaphysicians generally to start their treatises with the assertion that things seem, or are commonly thought, to be thus-and-thus, but turn out on reflection to be very different. The implication is that before we open such a treatise we have all sorts of naive beliefs, in the reliability of the senses, the existence of physical objects, the reality of change, the continuing identity of the self, the freedom of the will, to name only some of the more obvious. A first object of the metaphysician is to suggest that these beliefs, or some of them, have less foundation than is commonly supposed: if not precisely false, they are not wholly true, or not true of reality, or (to adapt a phrase of Bradley's already quoted) not true 'in their character as presented'. Sometimes, as in the case of Descartes, the attempt is made to show that we are wrong about the degree of conviction which should be attached to different classes of truths: we take it that propositions about things seen are clear and obvious and those about things unseen (God and the soul) far more doubtful, and it transpires that it is only the latter type of proposition that we can really be said to know. Sometimes, as with Hegel and Bradley, the more alarming claim is made that statements widely accepted by non-philosophers are not only not true of reality, but could not be, owing to internal contradictions in the concepts of which they consist. Change and time and relation, to mention three of the categories whose metaphysical adequacy is questioned by these writers, are said to contain ineradicable inconsistencies, with the result that nothing which falls under them can serve to express truth in the strict sense. It is added, however, that concepts of this kind, though not available for the characterization of real things, have a use of their own in qualifying appearances: they can be accepted as correct at their own level, even if this is not the metaphysical level.

Now it has long been customary to resist the more extravagant of these metaphysical paradoxes: to take an obvious example, the arguments propounded by Zeno and Parmenides with the object of showing the unreality of motion have seldom been found persuasive. But until very recently it was only on particular arguments of this kind that critics fastened their attention. The initial metaphysical premise, that there is an evident discrepancy between what is taken for granted by common sense and what philosophy shows to be true, excited no adverse comment, for it was a proposition to which the critics were themselves prepared to subscribe. Even Locke, the supposed philosopher of common sense, held that nature was very different from what it is commonly thought to be: the colours and smells which the plain man unhesitatingly attributes to the natural scene would not be there if all observers were removed, except potentially. His successor Hume certainly experienced no difficulty in reconciling antipathy to 'school' metaphysics with delight in paradox: despite an intermittent tendency to prefer the views of 'the Vulgar' to those of 'the Philosophers', it was on the side of the latter that he eventually came down. He was, after all, a philosopher himself, with his own strange tale to tell. Nor are the modern counterparts of the classical empiricists, such as Bertrand Russell and Rudolf Carnap, essentially different in this respect. In the case of Russell this is not perhaps surprising, seeing that much of his effort at the time of his greatest philosophical activity was devoted to saying what the world was really like, a task which presupposed the belief that it was not what it seemed to be. As for Carnap and his fellow Logical Positivists, they clearly thought the common man was in error at many points (over causal efficacy, for example, or again over belief in a continuing self-identical ego), though it was not to the metaphysician that they proposed to send him for correction.

But the situation about metaphysics and common sense is now totally changed. Thanks to the work of Moore and Wittgenstein, it is virtual orthodoxy that the very fact that a philosophical proposition could be true only if beliefs widely accepted by non-philosophers were rejected, or only if we abandoned ways of speaking which are constantly and successfully used, is a good and sufficient reason for thinking it false. That a philosopher should rest his assertions on paradox, i.e. on conflict with common sense or common usage, should certainly not be accounted to his credit, or even be allowed as venial; it should, on the contrary, be seen as fatal to his pretensions. Whether *any* positive philosophical pronouncements can be made if these stringent requirements are accepted is a serious question, but I shall not pursue it now. Instead, I wish to consider the case for common sense only so far as it bears on the possibility of metaphysics. That it has such a bearing will, I hope, be obvious, despite the fact that the elimination of metaphysics was not among the specific aims of its most prominent supporters. Moore, for all his criticisms of Bradley, never identified himself with the cause of Positivism, and Wittgenstein's preoccupation, in the period with which we are concerned, was with the things said by analytic philosophers, men who had professedly eschewed metaphysics. The effect of their work is, even so, profoundly anti-metaphysical, since it questions the legitimacy of what seems to be an essential initial move in the setting up of a metaphysical system. And it is the more necessary to consider it here in so far as it disputes the possibility of any kind of metaphysics, this-worldly as well as other-worldly. If our piecemeal knowledge is already everything it needs to be, we shall feel no call to proceed to *any* overall view of the world.

2. *Moore and common sense*

In what follows I shall concentrate first on the views of Moore, which are cruder than those of Wittgenstein but not for that reason uninstructive. From an early stage in his career Moore was preoccupied with the paradoxical character of many philosophical assertions and denials. He stated his own position on the point in a celebrated and influential essay, 'A Defence of Common Sense', first published in 1925. He began by laying down a long list of propositions which he himself described as 'truisms' and every one of which he said he *knew* to be true. Among these were (to use his own words):

> There exists at present a living human body, which is *my* body. This body was born at a certain time in the past, and has existed continuously ever since, though not without undergoing changes; it was, for instance, much smaller when it was born, and for some time afterwards, than it is now. Ever since it was born, it has been either in contact with or not far from the surface of the earth; and, at every moment since it was born, there have also existed many other things, having shape and size in three dimensions . . . from which it has been at various distances. . . . Among the things which have . . . formed part of its environment . . . there have . . . been large numbers of other living bodies. . . . Finally . . . , I am a

human being, and I have, at different times since my body was born, had many different experiences, of each of many different kinds. . . . And just as my body has been the body of a human being, namely myself, who has, during his lifetime, had many experiences . . . , so, in the case of very many of the other human bodies which have lived upon the earth, each has been the body of a different human being, who has, during the lifetime of that body, had many different experiences.[1]

Corresponding to each of these assertions by Moore about himself and his body are propositions which other living human beings would be prepared to assert about themselves and their bodies; and in each case, Moore says, they would say if asked that they quite certainly knew them to be true.

As will be obvious, the statements to whose truth Moore regards himself (and for that matter everyone else) as irrevocably committed are one and all concrete statements, about particular bodies, particular minds, the earth and so on. But it would be possible to formulate more abstract assertions corresponding to each broad division among them, and say, for instance, that *material objects are real* or that *there are other sentient beings in the universe besides myself*. The interest of this is that Moore thinks that the denial of each of these more general propositions would carry with it the denial of the *whole* class of particular propositions to which it corresponds. Conversely, to say we know that a particular proposition is true, for example that my body is now in contact with the surface of the earth, will entail rejecting the general proposition that there are no such things as material objects. At least two material objects, namely the earth and my body (if that can be properly classified as a material object), are *known* to exist. This example brings out the point of the whole procedure. Moore wants to point out the impossibility of simultaneously subscribing to a philosophical thesis like the thesis of idealism, that nothing exists except spirit, and persisting in the asseverations of everyday life. Given that we are sometimes correct in the latter (and on this point Moore says that none of us is in any real doubt), the falsity of the former immediately follows.

1. *Philosophical Papers*, pp. 33-4.

What we have here is an attempt to repudiate bold and far-reaching philosophical speculation on the ground that it conflicts with what everyone admits to be true when not engaged in philosophy, and thus flies in the face of common sense. That common sense is sometimes right, i.e. that there are everyday propositions which we know to be true, is taken as a datum. Moore admits that, if asked whether he really knows that the propositions in his list are true, he cannot do better than reply that it seems to him that he does know it, with certainty; he cannot prove that it is a matter of knowledge, as opposed to probability. But he is, all the same, quite adamant in rejecting the suggestion that their truth is in any way uncertain. The truisms he lists are, he declares, taken as absolutely true, not only by himself but by everyone. Even the philosophers who appear to maintain the contrary in fact admit them. They can deny them only for the sake of maintaining a thesis, and in one particular case the denial may even be self-stultifying, in so far as those who take the case for solipsism seriously show that they have no real belief in it by using the plural 'we' in stating their arguments. In so doing they seem to Moore 'constantly to betray the fact that . . . they regard the proposition that they themselves are not the only members of the human race, as not merely true, but *certainly* true'.[1]

As has already been mentioned, Moore's concern in putting forward these arguments is with philosophical assertions generally, as opposed to those of specifically metaphysical philosophers. But he would not of course have denied that they do apply to metaphysics, and indeed he used them himself to undermine metaphysical positions which were supported by his contemporaries, for example the thesis of idealism as stated above. It is a clear corollary of his view that metaphysicians must either accept what Moore calls 'the Common Sense view of the world' or spend their lives in the propagation of what they know to be evident falsehoods. There is no third alternative. Admittedly many metaphysicians try to have it both ways by saying of some of Moore's propositions that they are true in a certain sense, but false in another, or again by claiming that they are not 'ultimately' true, though perhaps true 'at a certain level'. Bradley, for example, held a view of this kind about temporal propositions. Time, he said, is not 'real': no statement containing a

1. *Philosophical Papers*, p. 43.

temporal expression can possible be true 'of reality'. But time for Bradley is none the less an 'appearance', and appearances, as he is never tired of insisting, one and all 'exist'. Moreover, whatever exists must in a certain way 'belong to reality'. I take this to mean that the temporal way of speaking is not wholly erroneous, i.e. that some propositions incorporating temporal expressions (and perhaps all significant propositions which answer this description) are partially true. But Moore professed to find this suggestion merely mystifying, evidence of nothing so much as Bradley's lack of candour, for it was his view that there are statements of the type in question which are known to be wholly and absolutely true. To describe them as partially true would be in effect to say that they were false, which (Moore said) they quite certainly were not.

Professor Morris Lazerowitz was so impressed by Moore's argument here that he maintained in his book *The Structure of Metaphysics* that there must be deep reasons why metaphysicians persisted in saying what they and everyone else knew to be false, and recommended recourse to psychoanalysis to uncover those reasons. But before resorting to so desperate an expedient we ought perhaps to try to sort out the issues between Moore and the philosophers he criticizes.

3. *Examination of Moore's views*

One such issue turns on whether the philosophers in question were meaning to affirm or deny any particular facts. Moore, as we have seen, was convinced that they were: to say, for example, that *material objects are not ultimately real* involved in his view denying that there are such things as the earth, the room in which I am now sitting, and so on. The persuasive force of the argument lay in the fact that these are just the things whose existence we all unhesitatingly acknowledge. But the philosophers Moore criticizes were scarcely wanting to say that it is wrong to hold that these things in particular exist, as opposed to other possible objects. They were not, that is to say, quarrelling with one individual judgment as against another, but rather questioning the value of a whole class of judgments. Given the legitimacy of the standpoint from which we speak of material objects, they would agree with Moore that e.g. the moon is real and the man in the moon imaginary. Their doubts concern not the correct application of the material object terminology, but rather its ultimate tenability.

It seems to me clear that this reply is correct, at least as regards intentions. But it is not a reply which would have satisfied Moore. For we can imagine him arguing that to raise doubts about the philosophical acceptability of a 'way of taking facts', to use a convenient phrase of Bradley's,[1] is precisely to ask whether any true statements can be made under this head, and pointing once more to universally acknowledged truths to clinch the issue. To distinguish, as was just done, between the correct application of a terminology and its 'ultimate tenability' is quite improper: unless it is 'ultimately tenable' it cannot have a correct application. So to suggest that, for instance, time is not real is to imply that all statements incorporating temporal expression are false, when we know very well they are not.

According to Moore and common sense, it is a fact that my body has existed continuously since I was born (and presumably for some time before that). According to Bradley and those who think like him, it is also a fact, though not perhaps an 'ultimate' fact. It should be clear that in the dispute between them much turns on the conception of fact, together with the associated conception of truth. And here there is a simple division of opinion between the two parties. When Moore says that something is a fact or that a statement is true or a matter of knowledge, he means that it is an ultimate fact or an absolutely true statement. Being a fact or being true are in this way of thinking all-or-nothing matters: a state of affairs either obtains or it does not, a statement is either true or it is not true. To describe a fact as provisional is in effect to admit that one does not know that it really is a fact. One cannot properly claim knowledge of something, the implication seems to be, without abandoning the right to change one's mind about it. Matters of knowledge are what they are eternally and timelessly (they are not dependent in any important way on the thinking of the persons in whose minds they actualize), and every truth is a final truth.

Bradley's assumptions on all these points could scarcely be more

1. *Appearance and Reality*, p. 218 (9th impression).

different. For one thing, he does not make the sharp separation which Moore does between fact and thinking. A fact for him is something asserted or judged to be the case; it is a conclusion to which we are driven as the result of a process of argument. We make up our minds about the facts in the light of available evidence; it is not a matter of simply discerning them. Admittedly some facts, including those mentioned by Moore, seem pretty obvious, but even here there can be no question of descrying isolated bits of the ultimate structure of the world. We cannot describe one situation in total isolation from another—the very fact that we use general terms precludes that—and any description we give will reflect both our previous experience and present assumptions. Hence any statement of fact must be subject to revision, though this does not mean that every such statement will at some time be revised. And though it is true that metaphysics, which claims to dispense with preconceptions of any sort, promises to provide an ultimate account of reality, as opposed to the special sciences, each of which works with principles which it does not justify, it is idle to suppose that it can reach such an account by taking over uncritically the most widely accepted beliefs of common sense. The pronouncements of common sense are no more exempt from philosophical scrutiny than any other sort of pronouncement.

This argument is by no means free from controversy; the role assigned to metaphysics as the arbiter of ultimate truth would certainly need prolonged consideration if our purpose now were to discuss it in full. Yet I think myself that we do not need to be in sympathy with the whole Bradleian position to feel the persuasiveness of its central point. The analysis of fact here put forward fits our everyday use of the term 'fact', as when we speak of the facts of science or of history, a good deal better than Moore's alternative account. What we take to be fact in these areas *is* subject to revision; facts here are not fixed for all time. Moore is of course right in arguing that we must not describe anything as a fact unless we are prepared to say we know it to be the case, and that we must not claim knowledge if any doubts about the matter linger in our minds. But it is one thing to say one has no doubts, and quite another to abandon the possibility of changing one's mind later. Moore's apparent identification of truth with final truth is strangely Platonic, and indeed his whole philosophy has at times the air of an odd sort of inverted Platonism. He may be said to subscribe to the Platonic account of knowledge as the sure and direct apprehension of a firm and unchangeable object; his difference from Plato is that he locates that object, except when it is a question of moral knowledge, in the familiar world. There is no need to rise to the apprehension of Forms to discover the nature of reality, since we already have sufficient knowledge of the truth at the mundane level. To Plato's dogma Moore thus opposes a counter-dogma of the same fundamental sort, setting the intuitions of common sense over against Plato's intuition of the supersensible. One wonders whether either sort of intuition has any part to play in a correct account of knowledge.

Moore perhaps makes a further assumption which is important for our present purposes. As well as taking it for granted that there are descriptions of states of affairs which can be known to be ultimately correct, he seems to assume further that to every state of affairs there corresponds only a single correct description. Conviction on this point would appear to lie behind his rejection of the view that the knowledge-claims of common sense must be subject to philosophical examination: the facts having severally been finally described, there is nothing for the sensible philosopher to do but accept the descriptions. This conclusion begins to look less plausible once we reflect that we can and do describe the same set of happenings from a variety of points of view and in a variety of different terminologies, and that the language we employ in such descriptions varies widely in sophistication and what may be called theoretical load. These are the conditions in which we naturally ask what is *really* happening and find ourselves grading different answers according to depth or superficiality. We recognize that a description can be, in a sense, perfectly correct and yet relatively unenlightening; it will do justice, in such circumstances, only to the surface show of things. The trouble about the deliverances of common sense is that they often are unenlightening in just this way. And the trouble with Moore as a critic of metaphysics is that he fails to take this factor into account. His conception of the appearance-reality dichotomy, which plays such a large part in metaphysical thought, is at bottom crude: he virtually identifies the real with the existent, and supposes that philosophical discussion about reality can be silenced by simply calling attention to what exists. Whether in the end we accept or reject the possibility of metaphysics, it seems clear that this short way with the question will not do.

It should be made clear that the above discussion is not intended to provide any positive endorsement of metaphysical claims. To point out that metaphysicians do not seek to dispute familiar facts, and therefore cannot be refuted by a straightforward reference to such facts, is not to show that they have a satisfactory alternative role. To make clear that the antithesis of appearance and reality is one we employ in real-life situations, thus disposing of the view that every true statement gives us *the* truth about reality, is to open up the way to philosophical reflection, but not necessarily to the sort of reflection which metaphysicians favour. It might be that the differences between contrasting descriptions were to be explained not, as the latter suppose, by invoking the notion of degrees of truth, but rather by a reference to different functions performed by the different descriptions: each will be adequate for its own purposes and none will give the final truth about things. The search for a description which is finally true and adequate for all purposes is on this view chimerical, and yet it is in this activity that metaphysicians appear to be engaged. We must accordingly turn now to consider the arguments advanced in support of this thesis, arguments developed with great power and persuasive force in the later writings of Wittgenstein.

4. *Wittgenstein as a metaphysician*

It is sometimes said that Wittgenstein himself was pursuing a metaphysical enquiry when he wrote his first book, the *Tractatus Logico-philosophicus*. He sought there to determine the conditions in which meaningful discourse is possible, being concerned in particular with the relations between what is said and the reality being talked about. It was in this connection that he introduced his distinction between 'atomic' and 'molecular' sentences or propositions. Molecular sentences, such as *All cats are fond of fish* or *Britain exports or dies*, were thought by Wittgenstein to be resolvable into atomic sentences joined by logical constants,[1] precisely as in logic compound formulae are taken to be truth-functions[1] of simple formulae. Just as the logician needs the notion of a simple or elementary statement-form,[1] commonly symbolized by single letters like p and q, in order to build up the complex formulae with which he is concerned, so Wittgenstein assumed at this stage that there must be atomic sentences if there is to be any meaningful discourse about the world. The function of an atomic sentence was to express the simplest kind of possible fact. Wittgenstein was greatly exercised by the question how the elements of a sentence of this kind could correspond to elements in reality; that there must be a precise correspondence if there was to be such a thing as truth or falsity seemed to him axiomatic. But, unlike Russell, who produced a similar theory about the same time, he offered no instances of atomic sentences or atomic facts; he was content to argue on general grounds that they must exist or obtain, and to point out that every such fact must of its nature be independent of all other facts of the same kind.

This system of ideas is described by modern critics as a metaphysics because in it Wittgenstein sought to determine what the world is like by reference to general, abstract or conceptual considerations. These considerations were derived by Wittgenstein from current logic, formal and philosophical. The preoccupation with the whole problem of meaning, and the attempt to give it a general solution, arose out of Frege's discussions of sense and reference, which had been taken up and continued by Russell. The distinction of atomic and molecular sentences, and the enterprising if scarcely successful project for treating the latter as truth-functions of the former, respectively came from and were encouraged by the formal logic to which Frege, Russell and Whitehead had given definitive expression. The procedure followed here is certainly analogous to that of other metaphysicians. Just as Aristotle began by determining in the abstract what was meant by the notion of substance, and Bradley by considering what conditions would have to be fulfilled if thought were to be truly comprehensive and coherent, so Wittgenstein took his start from reflection of the most general kind about meaning. There was perhaps a difference in so far as the thought of

1. Explanation of these terms can be found in the opening pages of any introductory textbook of symbolic logic.

Aristotle and Bradley rested in each case on a fundamental intuition of reality, whereas Wittgenstein did not move outside the austere confines of logic, but the argument was all the same identical in its formal nature.

Yet Aristotle and Bradley persisted in their metaphysics, whilst Wittgenstein repudiated his: the *Philosophical Investigations*[1] contain a detailed criticism of the central doctrines of the *Tractatus*,[2] and in doing so suggest new and subtle ways of attacking the whole metaphysical enterprise. We must now try to bring out what these are.

5. *Wittgenstein and Burke*

The most significant innovation in the later thought of Wittgenstein may be described as a move from abstract to concrete. In the *Tractatus*, as we have just seen, the problem of meaning was considered in a highly general way: Wittgenstein asked there what had to be true if there were to be meaningful discourse as such, and drew conclusions about the nature of the world from reflection on this topic. In the *Investigations*, by contrast, he started from the acknowledged fact that language is used meaningfully, and proceeded to investigate the ways in which it is given meaning. The central thought here was that there is not just one set of necessary conditions which has to be satisfied if language is to be used properly, but a whole series of related sets, each valid for a particular area of discourse. To use language is not to engage in a single, simple activity, but rather to embark on a plurality of activities which may resemble one another but are none the less each entitled to attention in its own right. There are many things we do with language, and many ways in which it can be successfully used. The right procedure for anyone who proposes to tackle the problem of meaning is accordingly to turn his attention to meaningful discourse as we have it, and to consider the wide variety of ways in which words are given meaning in what Wittgenstein called particular language games, i.e. particular areas of linguisitic activity. It is a profound mistake to think that a word or sentence has meaning in the abstract, though, in Wittgen-

1. Published posthumously in 1953.
2. Written during the war of 1914–18 and first published in 1921.

stein's view, it was a mistake made by almost all the philosophers who had discussed the subject, including himself when he wrote the *Tractatus*.

I mentioned earlier that there are certain points of comparison between the thought of Burke and Wittgenstein, and it may be useful to enlarge on this suggestion now. Burke was opposed to what he called the 'metaphysical' consideration of political problems: he thought it a gross error to begin, as so many of his contemporaries did, by laying down conditions which must be satisfied in any tolerable political society, e.g. respect for so-called natural rights. Instead of demanding that existing institutions conform to the requirements of abstract reason, the student of politics should recognize that the very fact that an institution exists is evidence of its rationality. To say that an institution exists is to say that men are prepared to adopt certain working arrangements in their dealings with each other; that they do so shows that a problem has been faced and solved. Admittedly, political institutions can become outmoded or cease to perform the functions for which they were designed; they need from time to time to be reformed, extended or even replaced. But the way to carry out the change, in Burke's view, is not to consult a blueprint for an ideal political society which exists nowhere, but to consider the problem concretely, as it affects a particular society. We need to recognize that the greater part of the complex structure of which the institution forms part must be in a healthy state, just because the people concerned are engaged in common political activities, and to confine reform to the relatively small area which is out of order. In effecting such reforms, moreover, it is of vital importance to have regard to the spirit and nature of existing institutions, the whole idea being to devise something which will continue to work effectively. The last thing the reformer should imagine is that he might wipe out the whole of an existing structure and begin again from first principles. Nor is it a question here only of what is practical, but also of what is reasonable. The rational course in politics is to see that any arrangement which works has reason in it, and can accordingly be set aside only at the risk of substantial loss.

Wittgenstein's attitude to language in his later philosophy shows many parallels to this. First and most important, he was convinced that language should be treated as a viable working institution, or rather a series of such institutions. Language, as he repeatedly stressed, is a social phenomenon, a co-operative achievement; the idea of a purely private language is an absurdity. The very fact that people engage in linguistic activities, knowing what to say or reply in particular contexts, is evidence that those activities are in order as they stand. To consider language from the outside, and presume to judge it by first principles of a necessarily abstract character, was wholly mistaken. To pronounce about language in general, as philosophers had sought to do, was to engage in an activity at once one-sided and misleading, one-sided because any such pronouncement must be based on a survey of a restricted range of examples, misleading because of the dogmatism it encouraged. The only rational course for the student of language was to recognize the multifarious nature of linguistic phenomena as we actually meet them in real life, and to insist against the prematurely generalizing philosopher that attention be paid to this diversity. And what needed to be observed in this connection was not only that the meaning of individual words and phrases varied according to the different contexts in which they occurred, but also that the purposes to which language is put are extraordinarily diverse. To take one use of language—what is sometimes rather vaguely described as the descriptive use—as the standard one and discuss meaning with exclusive reference to it, as so many philosophers did, was to ignore the most obvious facts.

6. Wittgenstein as a metaphysical neutralist

The bearing of these arguments on metaphysics can now be made clear. In our preceding discussion we represented the metaphysician as one who promises an account of experience which is at once coherent and comprehensive. And we argued that one circumstance which prompts people to seek such an account is the fact that apparently conflicting things can be said of a single situation. The scientist, the theologian, the moralist may all have their comment to make, and when one ascribes a result to gland deficiencies, a second to defects of character and a third to the displeasure of God at the sinful nature of men, it is natural to enquire which can be said to have the truth of the matter. The assumption here is that each of the different persons concerned is at bottom engaged on the same task: he is seeking to characterize and explain what is going on. It is at this point that Wittgenstein's reflections on language become relevant. For Wittgenstein stresses, first, that any comment which is made in what may be called a live linguistic situation, as part of a language game which is actually played, must be in order as it is, so that there can be no question of dismissing it out of hand as improper, and secondly that the belief that all the speakers in a situation like the one described are occupied in the same task, namely saying how things are, is quite unfounded. Instead of trying to decide between the different parties, or to produce some sort of synthesis of what they all say, we should accordingly concern ourselves with the question what each intends to do in saying what he does. And if we do that the result can only be that the presumed conflict is seen to disappear, for it emerges that the point of the different utterances is by no means the same. So far from being rivals the speakers are complementary, and there can no more be a question of choosing between or reconciling them than there can of choosing between or reconciling the activities of cricketers and baseball players.

This _neutralist_ attitude to the problem of metaphysics, as it may well be called, is not new. It was adopted in a restricted form by Kant in his solution of the third Antinomy, and it may be useful to explore his use of it there both to illustrate the general idea and as a basis for subsequent comment.

The third Antinomy arises out of the conflict of two diverse metaphysical views, to which Kant gives the curious names 'Epicureanism' and 'Platonism'. The first maintains, on the evidence of the achievements of the natural sciences, that there is nothing in the world which is exempt from natural necessity. Everything that happens does so because of what has previously happened; every event is determined to be what it is. Against this the 'Platonist' wants to say that there are at least some happenings which need not have been what they in fact are, namely those which are due to human agency, adducing as evidence the fact that people are praised and blamed for what they do, and maintaining that praise and blame do not make sense unless those to whom they are ascribed could have done otherwise than they did.

There seems to be a head-on conflict between the parties here, but Kant insists that it is not a real one. What makes it unreal, in his view, is the diversity of the bases on which the two views rest. The 'Epicurean', as we saw, rests his case on the scientist's conviction that all events in nature are determined, whilst the 'Platonist' appeals to the moral ascription of praise and blame as quite inconsistent with this. But the purpose of the scientist's activity is to understand and explain, whereas that of the moral agent is to get things done or prevent them coming about. The one stands outside the world; his attitude is that of a simple spectator. The whole interest of the other is in action: he needs not to contemplate the world but to intervene in it. And the utterances and concepts of the two must be judged by reference to their respective purposes and points of view. To take up the moral standpoint and assess actions as worthy of praise and blame is, normally at any rate, a legitimate proceeding, but we must not imagine that we thereby add to our understanding of the world. The whole point of a moral judgment is practical, whereas the whole point of scientific statement is theoretical. Kant emphasizes this divergency in a dubious way which connects with the rest of his philosophy by saying that the standpoint of the scientist is 'phenomenal' and that of the moralist 'noumenal'; a person who is faced with the necessity of acting may be said to adopt the 'noumenal' point of view. But it is not necessary to take this terminology seriously to see sense in the whole idea.

The strength of Kant's solution of the free-will problem, which has had many modern imitators, lies in his attempt to do justice to the claims of both morals and science. He felt in his bones that neither could be set aside, and one of his principal arguments for his own 'critical' point of view was that only on it could the rights of both be preserved. But it must be admitted that he had no formal or general case to advance against setting one or the other aside. Wittgenstein undoubtedly made an advance on Kant not merely in generalizing his procedure, but also in producing his concept of language as a viable institution, entitled to respect just because it is successfully used. His enigmatic notion of a 'form of life', a recognizable area of human activity which we cannot seriously think away, is also of importance in this connection.

7. *Language games and theoretical commitment*

Does Wittgenstein really carry conviction against the would-be metaphysician? The answer to this question depends on how far we are prepared to accept his view about the independence of the various language games in which we take part. According to the strict letter of the theory, each such game is played according to its own rules and for its own purposes, and none enjoys priority in any real sense over any other. In particular, the game or games in which we say or explain how things are is in no sense more fundamental than other linguistic activities. We are concerned here only with one use of language, not with an all-important central use.

It seems to me that this contention might well be questioned. I should not deny, of course, that there are many distinct kinds of linguistic activity; issuing an order, expressing a request, uttering a prayer and pronouncing a sentence in court are all very different from each other as well as from describing and explaining what is the case. Nor should I wish to say that the last-named was historically the first of men's linguistic achievements: language was doubtless employed to threaten or frighten before it was used for communication. Yet it remains true that there is a sense in which a theoretical commitment is involved in non-theoretical uses of language. Take prayer as an instance. A man who prays to the god of the sea for a safe voyage before embarking is committed to the belief that there is such a god, and further that whether or not he arrives safely depends, or may depend, on the god's decision; if these beliefs are false the whole procedure is invalidated. To pray is certainly not to say what is the case, but it is to imply what is the case. And if the implication is one which there is no reason to accept, there will be little point in insisting that the forms in which prayers of this sort are offered are widely recognized and acted upon. It may be that this particular language game is played, but if it is played on false pretences we need not be impressed by that fact. Nor again will it be germane to point out that prayer has its uses even in circumstances where the object to which it is addressed is non-existent: it serves to comfort and encourage the worshipper, if nothing else. Institutions and activities can certainly serve other purposes than those for which they were designed, but the fact that they develop in this way, though of great interest to the student of human nature or human societies, is scarcely of concern to the metaphysician, who must necessarily take them at their face value and with their original pretensions. In doing so he is, after all, only following the lead of those who belong to the institutions concerned, few if any of whom would be prepared to abandon as unimportant the theoretical assumptions to which they are committed on a straightforward interpretation of their behaviour.

I have taken as an instance a practice more commonly found in the ancient than the modern world, but I want to insist that the problem it raises is by no means unique to prayer in a primitive setting. Exactly the same questions can be asked about prayer of any kind, and indeed about religious discourse generally. The purposes which such discourse serves may well be practical rather than theoretical, but this does not take away from the fact that it proceeds on a presupposition about fact, the falsity of which would render the whole procedure invalid. To put it crudely, unless God really exists religious language does not make proper sense. To show that it makes internal sense, i.e. that there is agreement among those who practise it in the concepts they employ, will not be sufficient as an answer to this contention.

A distinguished follower of Wittgenstein, Professor Norman Malcolm, in effect took this line in a striking article on the Onto-logical Argument,[1] in which he argued that attention to the concept of God as it figured in actual religious discourse, for example in the 90th Psalm, showed that God was there conceived as a being to whom existence belonged necessarily. For Professor Malcolm this fact was all-important; no considerations of general logic or philo-sophical assumptions about existence could set it aside. Malcolm performed a major service here in showing that the Ontological Argument is not, as philosophers have too readily supposed, the product of a simple logical muddle, but is rather an attempt to explicate a notion which is taken seriously in a most important area of human activity. But to make this point is not, as he seems to imagine, to settle a problem but rather to set one: we are confronted with the task of saying how we can reconcile our ordinary assump-

1. *Philosophical Review*, 1960.

tions about existence with what is involved in this particular region of discourse. To assure ourselves that our concept of God is not only widely accepted but also legitimate we have to produce a connected and coherent account of the diverse sides of experience. But this is exactly what metaphysics proposes to do.

Precisely the same considerations apply to Kant's solution of the third Antinomy. Kant seeks to dissolve the conflict by pointing out that moral judgments are practical and scientific judgments theoretical; he hopes in this way to arrange for their peaceful coexistence. We can be determinists as observers and nevertheless adopt a wholly different point of view when we act.

The trouble about this is that moral practice itself proceeds on assumptions whose correctness cannot simply be taken as self-evident: we have to ask ourselves, in the light of the findings of the natural and social sciences, whether we can persist in the view that, in many everyday situations, men could have acted otherwise than they did. If Kant and his modern followers like Professor Ryle were right, no scientific discoveries would be relevant to the free-will issue, for we should know in advance that science is concerned with what is and morals with what ought to be.

It hardly seems true that this is how we actually think about the matter. The acceptance of psychological findings has profoundly modified thought about criminal responsibility: the idea that the average criminal is in any real sense free to act otherwise is certainly much less plausible than it was. The introduction of the concept of diminished responsibility into English law would also seem to be due to recognition of the extent to which people's behaviour depends on factors outside their control.

Admittedly, neither of these points is decisive, for a Kantian could reply that what has transpired is that we have narrowed the application of some of our common moral concepts, without abandoning them altogether. It remains true, nevertheless, that the deterministic overtones of the social sciences have a way of spreading beyond the bounds inside which orthodox thinkers would like to keep them; in an atmosphere where we are constantly extending the range of persons about whom talk of social conditioning seems appropriate it is hard to keep up with the full rigour of older ways of thought. If it is an exaggeration to suggest that moral praise and blame are on their way out, as a result of scientific discoveries, it is very much less of an exaggeration than it would have been at the beginning of the century. There is at least a threat here that a language game which is played now may cease to be played, or again may be played in a highly modified form; possibilities which are not much considered in current discussions of the subject.

8. Metaphysics and 'ordinary language'

To what extent is such a threat at all genuine? There are philosophers who would certainly regard it as idle, and we must now consider the grounds on which they would rest their view.

One way of supporting the position can be arrived at by generalizing an argument of Professor Malcolm's. In his paper on 'Moore and Ordinary Language'[1] Malcolm put forward a linguistic version of Moore's defence of common sense. He argued that if an expression has a use in ordinary, i.e. non-philosophical, language, that very fact may be taken as exempting it from philosophical criticism, for actual use implies proper use. Malcolm was perhaps thinking primarily of the descriptive use of language, since he was concerned, like Moore, with Bradley's denial of the reality of time. But what he said could be given a wider significance if it were taken to cover uses of language of every sort. The point would then be that the fact that people have a use for expressions like 'He did it of his own free will' or 'Guilty but insane' is enough to authenticate the concepts concerned. And the case seems even stronger when it is pointed out that we have to do in actual fact not with single expressions, as in the instances given, but with elaborately connected sets of expressions. That a single phrase should be systematically misused is perhaps just thinkable, but it is quite another thing to suggest that the same might be true of a whole area of discourse, with all the fine distinctions there involved.

Yet this argument, when we come to think about it, can be seen to introduce no new point of principle. Its strength lies in its Burkeian emphasis on the complex structure of an existing institution, with the implication that such an institution is entitled to respect just

1. In *The Philosophy of G. E. Moore*, ed. P. A. Schilpp (1942), pp. 343 ff.

because it is accepted. This is a good point to make against wholesale reformers, whether in the sphere of language or in that of politics, but not one which could effectively silence a really determined critic. For what is being said here, after all, is no more than is embodied in the Wittgensteinian dictum 'This game is played'; the argument, at bottom, is once more from successful use to valid use. And the difficulty about this is that there is no absurdity in raising doubts about the validity of uses of language which are entirely successful in the sense of agreed and acted upon. We do this in a trivial instance when we question the meaningful character of what is said at spiritualist *séances*, despite the fairly elaborate vocabulary there employed; we do it altogether more seriously when we wonder whether there really is anything in religion. A doubter on such a point is no more likely to be assured by having his attention directed to the whole language of religion and theology than was a critic of the *ancien régime* by Burke's insisting that it was and long had been a going concern.

It may still be felt, despite all the critic can say, that the main forms of life are fixed and abiding, and thus that Malcolm's argument is unassailable in practice if not in principle. Can we imagine ourselves abandoning, say, the language and procedures of the law, or the subtle methods developed in everyday discourse to exonerate and excuse when the plain imputation of a fault seems too harsh? Could any philosophical considerations persuade us that the whole of science is a fraud, or that there is no truth in history? But even if it were admitted that the answer to all such questions is negative (and it is not clear that the negative would be equally firm in every case), this would not dispose of the problem of thinking out the basis on which apparently disparate forms of life can coexist. Once it is allowed that every major human activity rests on a theoretical claim, the need for an overall view of the world becomes urgent. That many quite intelligent people manage to get along without such a view is no reason for denying the propriety of trying to arrive at one if we can.

There is another point which is worth stressing in this connection. Suppose it were agreed that the main forms of life are fixed: there might still be a question about the value to be assigned to one as against another. In one sense it must be allowed that law and science are facts, permanent features of the human scene. But they are facts which can be taken in very different ways. The valuation put upon them by their exponents will not necessarily be shared by outsiders; there will always be critics who say that law is nothing but a crude practical device, indispensable perhaps but of its nature fundamentally unjust, and science a purveyor of almost meaningless abstractions. One of the attractions of the British Idealists, for many persons in their own generation and for some since, lay in the fact that they tried to rationalize and justify the attitude behind these judgments. Nor do we need to share this attitude to believe that the issues raised are serious. A materialist should recognize their importance as readily as an idealist. And though application of the techniques of critical philosophy will go a long way to clarify the problems involved, I do not myself believe that it will remove all difficulties. Crude as it may seem to put it this way, we have in the end to make up our minds whether we are for or against science, and to do it on the basis of a general philosophical view. To work out such a view is the task of the metaphysician.

I am inclined for these reasons to think Wittgenstein's implied criticism of metaphysics no more effective than Moore's. Both make points of great interest, whose importance has been insufficiently appreciated by philosophical reformers; each draws attention to paradoxes and hazards to which we are committed if we embark on the metaphysical enterprise. Wittgenstein's emphasis on language as an institution was in its context as salutary as Burke's appeal to the rationality of the *status quo* in politics. Yet just as Burke fails to persuade us that we need no general theory of politics, but only histories of particular political institutions, so Wittgenstein's advocacy of the view that we should confine ourselves to particular language games does not satisfy. Not all language games, we feel, are equally well founded, even if they are all played. And we have recourse to metaphysics to try to grapple with the difficulties raised by that fact.

9

The Origins of Hegelianism

1. *Metaphysics and bad logic*

HOW DO metaphysical systems arise? We have already seen that there is a certain disagreement among critics of metaphysics about the proper answer to this question. An answer which is still widely favoured finds the origin of metaphysics in bad logic, or, more plausibly, in a combination of bad logic and wishful thinking. It is alleged that the metaphysician wants to believe a certain conclusion, that he has no real ground for drawing it, but that he nevertheless cajoles himself and his readers into accepting it by logical sleight of hand. Parmenides is on this view a prime example of the metaphysical thinker, since it was on the logical principles of identity and contradiction that his whole strange account of 'what is' was built up. Taking the principle of identity to assert that if a thing has a property it must have that property eternally, and the principle of contradiction to preclude the possibility that a thing could have a property at one time and not have it at another, Parmenides went on to deduce that 'what is' is altogether different from what it is commonly taken to be, since it is entirely immobile and totally exempt from change. According to the critics we are considering, there was nothing wrong with the deduction in this case; it was faulty logical premises which led to the paradoxical result.

The foregoing discussions do not suggest that this account will have general application, whatever its plausibility in the case of Parmenides (the background to whose philosophizing is, as it happens, almost unknown). Nor is its acceptance encouraged by the reflection that those who put it forward have, as was remarked earlier, little or no personal sympathy with metaphysics, and indeed are committed by the general principles of their philosophy to the conclusion that metaphysical pronouncements, being neither empirical nor analytic, cannot make sense. That they should offer an external reconstruction of metaphysical thinking, rather than exhibit it from the inside, is in the circumstances not surprising. And that external reconstruction of this kind may miss the point, revealing the mechanics of a system but leaving out what gives it life, has, as we have seen, been suggested even in the case of the Ontological Argument, which is, on the face of it, as good an example of metaphysical thinking on the Positivist model as could be imagined.

Instead of debating these issues further in a general way, I propose now to investigate the origins of a particular metaphysical system in some detail. The system I have chosen is that of Hegel. Hegel is peculiarly suitable as a subject for this enquiry: because of his wide-ranging ambitions and general reputation as a speculative philosopher; because he seems to the unsympathetic to display all the typical vices of metaphysicians—obscurity, logical slovenliness, shameless equivocation; finally and by no means least important, because his early philosophical development is exceptionally well documented. Thanks to the survival of some of his early notebooks we can see his thought in the making and trace the main stages by which his first crude ideas were transformed until they took on the characteristic shape we associate with Hegelianism. In what follows I shall be occupied with just this task.

2. *Hegel's earliest writings*

Hegel was born in 1770 and his first surviving philosophical writings are from the period 1793–1800. First published by Hermann Nohl in 1907 under the title *Hegels theologische Jugendschriften*, they fall into five main parts. There is first of all a series of fragments which date from 1793 or soon after and whose main subject is the notion of a '*Volksreligion*' or popular religion. Next comes a short life of Jesus, which dates from 1795. Third in the volume is a longer, incomplete essay to which Nohl gave the title 'The Positivity of the Christian Religion', most of which dates from 1795–6. Fourth comes the masterpiece of the collection, a virtually complete treatise which

Nohl called 'The Spirit of Christianity and its Fate', written in 1798 or 1799. Finally there are a number of fragments or drafts from the end of the period, including two isolated bits of what must have been a substantial work written in 1800 and entitled by Nohl 'Fragment of a System'. None of this material, it must be emphasized, was published by Hegel himself; there is, indeed, no evidence that he intended to publish any of it. The indications are rather that he wrote with the primary intention of clarifying his own mind. It follows that we need to show special caution in interpretation in dealing with this work, the more so because of Hegel's tendency, familiar enough in his main writings, to explore philosophical positions in a dialectical manner, i.e. to work them out as if he were in full agreement with them, although intending eventually to turn round and repudiate them. We cannot assume that Hegel positively identified himself with all the points of view which are expressed in Nohl's volume. But though this makes it difficult to be certain about all the details of his philosophical development, it does not affect the main outlines.

3. Objective religion, 'positivity', the Jews

I begin with some brief remarks about the earliest fragments. On pp. 6–7 of Nohl's collection we find Hegel giving what he calls 'an exposition of the difference between objective and subjective religion'. Objective religion is, roughly, the religion of the head, subjective religion the religion of the heart. Objective religion is associated with the intellect, the memory, the appeal to fear and with sectarianism and the elaboration of a dogmatic theology; subjective religion is, by contrast, non-theological. Subjective religion shows itself in the spirit in which a man acts. It is the same the world over, for differences of creeds are inessential. The heathen, 'as people call them',[1] can be as religious in this sense as any Christian. Hegel quotes from the well-known work of Lessing, *Nathan the Wise*, frequently in support of this point.

This crude contrast is developed on a basis which is essentially Kantian, as the frequent mention of 'practical reason' shows. But

1. Nohl, 10.

it is interesting to observe that even at this stage Hegel was proposing amendments to Kant. In a passage[1] discussing moral psychology he singles out qualities like sympathy, kindliness, friendship from the other passions and, while allowing that they have no moral worth in themselves and are, as Kant said, 'empirical' and therefore unstable, maintains that they nevertheless hinder men's bad inclinations and further the best in them. Moral feeling itself, Hegel adds, belongs to this sphere, whose fundamental principle is love. Love is a sort of analogon of reason: just as reason as citizen of an intelligible world recognizes itself in other individuals, so is love too directed outwards and finds itself, or rather forgets itself, in others. Love is an empirical factor; it is, as Kant had said, 'pathological', but it is emphatically not selfish. In acting on principles of love we are not hoping to get ourselves greater or more enduring pleasures than we should if we indulged our other inclinations.

The concept of love, as we shall see, was to play a large part in Hegel's early thought. The notion of a 'Volksreligion', developed in the immediately following pages, does not appear under the same name again. By a 'Volksreligion' Hegel means originally no more than a public religion of a satisfactory type, and it is obvious from his remarks that what he had in mind was something like the civic religion of the Greek city states. He mentions in one passage[2] three features which we should expect such a religion to have. First, its teachings must be based on universal reason as opposed to authority, and it must be possible for the simplest minds to follow them. Second, 'imagination, the heart and sensibility' must be given their due in it, a result which can be produced partly by the judicious use of ceremonies, partly by the construction and propagation of myths (presumably like the myths of the Greek gods). Third, it must be so devised that 'all needs of life—public political acts—connect with it'. In this third requirement Hegel has in mind both the restricted character of official Christianity as he knew it—its failure to touch all aspects of life—and its open hostility to many activities in which ordinary men find pleasure. 'The popular festivals of the Greeks', he observes,[3] 'were all religious festivals', and this is a state of affairs he would like to see reproduced. He remarks in the same context that the 'spirit of a people, its history, religion and the degree of its

1. Nohl, 18 ff.   2. Nohl, 20 ff.   3. Nohl, 27.

political freedom cannot be treated separately from one another'
and again that '*Volksreligion* and freedom go hand in hand'. A
community whose religious life is unsatisfactory is liable to be unsatisfactory through and through.

What is remarkable about these speculations is not so much their
positive content, which is obviously immature, however much it
prefigures some of Hegel's later doctrines, as the intellectual independence of their author, an independence which is strikingly, indeed startlingly, shown in a series of comparisons[1] between Socrates
and Jesus, very much to the advantage of Socrates. The more finished
works which follow, the 'Life of Jesus' and the essay on 'The
Positivity of the Christian Religion', are almost tame and conven-
tional by contrast. In both Hegel speaks as one who has swallowed
Kantian ethics, if not quite whole, at any rate very substan-
tially; in both his general attitude is that of a man of the Enlightenment.

The 'Life' presents Jesus speaking the language of Kant and re-
calling men from the darkness of contemporary religious practices
to awareness of the spark of reason within them; its tone is starkly
rationalistic, all mention of the Virgin Birth and the Resurrection
being omitted, along with miracles and stories of healings. Jesus is
a simple man with a simple message, the message that the spirit is
supremely important and the letter supremely unimportant. His aim
is to remind his countrymen of what is at present hidden under a
welter of meaningless forms and usages. He fails because the dead
weight of Jewish tradition is too strong for him.

In the essay on positivity too Jesus is the teacher of what Hegel
calls a 'virtue religion', something which contrasts sharply with the
religion of the Jews, and the problem of the essay is stated[2] as being
to understand how a teacher like Jesus could have 'afforded any
inducement to the creation of a positive religion, i.e. a religion which
is grounded in authority and puts men's worth not at all, or at least
not wholly, in morals'. Christianity was originally, on this view of
the matter, nothing more than the recommendation of a 'free
virtue springing from man's own being'; it has since become a

1. Nohl, 33 ff.
2. *Hegel's Early Theological Writings*, translated by T. M. Knox, p. 71;
Nohl, 155.

series of doctrines received on authority and professed by a restricted sect conscious of its own separation from the rest of the world.

Hegel traces the beginnings of this degeneration to the conditions in which Jesus taught. Because he was a Jew himself and had to accommodate himself to the expectations and prejudices of the Jews, Jesus had to lay stress on his own personality, and this feature was misunderstood by his disciples who 'had not attained truth and freedom by their own exertions; only by laborious learning had they acquired a dim sense of them and certain formulas about them. Their ambition was to grasp and keep this doctrine faithfully and to transmit it equally faithfully to others without any addition, without letting it acquire any variations in detail by working on it themselves'.[1] The subsequent expansion of the Christian community increased the emphasis on faith and belief, as opposed to respect for a man's free judgment, with the end result that the church became authoritarian not only in respect of its own members, but over the whole sphere of social and political life. Against this invasion of the rights of man by (the wrong sort of) religion Hegel protests as emphatically as any eighteenth-century *Aufklaerer*.

Among the most striking features of the two works we are considering is an extremely hostile characterization of the religious and moral life of the ancient Jews. Hegel's attitude to the Jews (which was not one of simple anti-semitism) is one of the few constant factors in his thought during these formative years. He saw Jewish life as a matter of unquestioning obedience to authority, authority whose regulations professed to cover every aspect of human activity. The following passage from the beginning of the 'Positivity' essay will illustrate points he made over and over again:

> The Jews were a people who derived their legislation from the supreme wisdom on high and whose spirit was now [i.e. in the time of Jesus] overwhelmed with a burden of statutory commands which pedantically prescribed a rule for every casual action of daily life and gave the whole people the look of a monastic order. As a result of this system, the holiest of things, namely the service of God and virtue, was ordered and compressed in dead formulas,

1. Knox, 81; Nohl, 162–3.

and nothing save pride in this slavish obedience to laws not laid down by themselves was left to the Jewish spirit.[1]

Jewish life, in short, was dominated by the relationship of master and slave, the Jews being slaves to their far-off and wholly transcendent God; it was through and through legalistic; it involved a denial of the free spirit of man and what Hegel called[2] a 'monkish preoccupation with petty, mechanical, spiritless and trivial usages'.

In thinking about the problems of morals and religion in his early years Hegel had the case of the Jews, to which he saw many parallels in modern society, constantly before his mind: terms like 'slavish', 'mechanical', 'lifeless' became regular parts of his vocabulary of abuse. What is more interesting, he came shortly to transfer the things he said about Jewish life to something very different, namely the operations of the intellect, which he saw as equally preoccupied with dead (abstract) formulae and equally incapable of doing justice to living spirit. Hegel's criticism of the Jews was thus the earliest version of his celebrated polemic against the scientific understanding, the first step in the working out of the negative aspect of his dialectic.[3]

4. Morality of rules and morality of love

This, however, is to anticipate. If we turn to the opening sections of 'The Spirit of Christianity', the most mature and the most strikingly original of the works in Nohl's collection, we find that Hegel's interests are still predominantly practical. He is concerned, that is to say, primarily with the question what would be a satisfactory form

1. Knox, 68–9; Nohl, 153.
2. Knox, 69; Nohl, 153.
3. In his mature philosophy Hegel distinguished within the human intellect between the faculty of understanding, which is in his view clear but remote from life, and that of philosophical reason, which thinks concretely or 'dialectically'. He was obviously moving towards this antithesis in his early writings, but he did not make it there, and the terms 'intellect', 'understanding', 'reflection', which are roughly synonymous, all carry pejorative overtones at this stage. 'Reason' in the early writings usually signifies Kant's practical reason, as in the passage quoted on pp. 143–4.

of human society, rather than with what would be a satisfactory
form of thought. He begins once more from the Jews, whose tragic
history is analysed in detail. I will mention here only what is said of
Abraham, whose ambition it was, we are told,[1] to be 'a wholly subsistent, independent man', and who sought to realize it by a policy
of mastery of nature combined with the maximum possible withdrawal from human relationships. Abraham, says Hegel,[2] was 'a
stranger on earth, a stranger to the soil and to men alike', living a
loveless and unlovely life. Abraham on this account is in fact the
prototype of what was later to be called the abstract universal, the
one which maintains itself by excluding differences, as opposed to
the concrete universal which is self-differentiating and does not
merely stand over against the many but enriches itself by actively
including them.

The fate of the Jewish people, uncharitably compared by Hegel
to the fate of Macbeth, was set by Abraham and consolidated in the
legislation of Moses, who freed the Jews from one yoke only to lay
on them another. It was against the effects and working of this
legislation that the whole life of Jesus was a protest, and Hegel proceeds to an exposition of the teaching of the gospels with the primary
object of showing how Jesus overcame legalism. Here, of course, we
meet with a theme he had treated before, both in the 'Life' and in the
essay on 'Positivity'; but the details of the new treatment are
strikingly different. The difference can be put crudely by saying that
whereas in the works written around 1795 Hegel's Jesus was a
Kantian character, urging men to use their own judgment in moral
matters instead of passively surrendering to authority, he has in
'The Spirit of Christianity' broken with Kant and developed a
positive moral standpoint of his own. The answer to legalism can no
longer be found by having recourse to the doctrine of the autonomy
of the will, for the whole Kantian set-up, when we look at it closely,
turns out to embody a legalism of its own. A true philosophy of
spirit must accordingly go beyond Kant and preach not a morality
of rules, but a morality of love.

I must now try to explain and document these points. Hegel puts
out his argument in the form of a commentary on Christian teaching, in particular the teaching of the Sermon on the Mount. Some of

1. Knox, 185; Nohl, 245.   2. Knox, 186; Nohl, 246.

this he represents as being utterly antithetical to Jewish belief. Thus[1] 'over against commands which required a bare service of the Lord, a direct slavery, an obedience without joy, without pleasure or love, i.e. the commands in connection with the service of God, Jesus set their precise opposite, a human urge and so a human need'. The reference is to Jesus' attitude to the Sabbath, which Hegel regards as deliberately provocative. Elsewhere, however, he portrays Jesus as developing rather than destroying what went before; the gospel phrase about 'fulfilling the law' is much invoked in this connection. The Sermon on the Mount was 'an attempt, elaborated in numerous examples, to strip the laws of legality, of their legal form'[2] and in it Jesus displayed 'a spirit raised above morality'. The laws in question are those which 'from varying points of view we call either moral or else civil commands'.[3] Hegel maintains that, in urging us to accept these laws in a new spirit, Jesus was in effect abolishing their sheerly objective character, getting rid in them of the element of pure command. And what makes his contention of particular interest is that he extends his condemnation (or rather says Jesus extended it) beyond the mere acceptance of a moral rule on someone else's authority to the acceptance of moral rules of any sort. A man who listens to the commands of duty is at bottom no better off than one who blindly accepts the Mosaic law. Kant, for all his denunciation of heteronomy of the will, merely set up the relationship of mastery and slavery inside a man instead of outside him. 'For the particular— impulses, inclinations, pathological love, sensuous experience, or whatever it is called—the universal is necessarily and always something alien and objective'.[4] Kantian ethics, for that matter, are unsatisfactory in other respects too, above all in suggesting that the good life can be comprehended in a series of formulae which we have only to observe in order to do all that could possibly be asked of us.

But how, we may well ask, could anyone expect to get beyond the Kantian point of view and still preserve morality? How could the element of command be eliminated from the moral life? We can distinguish three main points in Hegel's answer to these all-important questions. First, we must give up thinking of the moral life as a

1. Knox, 206; Nohl, 262.   2. Knox, 212; Nohl, 266.
3. Knox, 209; Nohl, 264.   4. Knox, 211; Nohl, 266.

constant struggle between duty and inclination. A man is not satisfactorily represented as a compound of warring elements, flesh and
spirit, which are utterly alien to each other. When we act in the spirit
of love as opposed to on the motive of duty we are not, despite Kant,
obeying an impulse which is 'pathological': in such circumstances
reason and inclination are in harmony, and instead of 'the domina-
tion of the concept', declaring itself in a 'Thou shalt', we have 'by
contrast an "is", a modification of life'.[1] This issues secondly in an
altogether different attitude to morality, an attitude which Hegel
describes in one place[2] as 'elevation above the sphere of rights,
justice, equity'. The truly moral man, as opposed to the Kantian,
will not think about what is due to him or what it would be fair for
him or others to have: he will not stand on his rights, but act out of
'a righteousness of a new kind';[3] in other words, out of love. This
will mean, thirdly, that he will not think that moral truth can be
comprehended in a set of general formulae, but will rather treat
particular situations on their merits, trying to judge the persons
concerned in them as individuals rather than types or cases. Hegel
claims[4] that the actions of men who work in this way 'when judged
by laws and moral imperatives, are found to be in accordance with
these', but it is not clear how he would justify this. If, for example,
we thought it right to treat moral backsliding with severity we should
not find it easy to accept the judgment recommended in the parable
of the Prodigal Son.

Questions could clearly be asked about the accuracy of Hegel's
portrayal of the morality of the Sermon on the Mount, and again
about the fairness of the criticisms he brings against Kantian ethics;
I cannot pursue such questions here. Nor can I give details of the
long, and on the whole unconvincing, treatment of the notions of
punishment and fate which follows the passages just analysed, in
which Hegel seems to say that the Greek idea of a man bringing a
fate upon himself through his own deeds is morally superior to that
which governs a punishment situation where the offender stands
irreconcilably under the control of something alien. The main theme
here is obviously identical with that of the section on morality of
love, but the way it is worked out is in this case bafflingly obscure.

1. Knox, 212; Nohl, 266.   2. Knox, 222; Nohl, 274.
3. Knox, 214; Nohl, 267.   4. Knox, 219; Nohl, 271–2.

Fortunately the ideas we have examined provide a sufficient illustration of the lines along which Hegel's thought was developing. The notion of a morality of love, in which law and inclination are reconciled, and the oppositions between objective and subjective, universal and particular, are overcome, not only anticipates some of the main features of Hegel's mature ethics, but has implications for his metaphysics too. Its use here shows how the idea of a non-formalistic 'dialectical' logic was originally tried out in another sphere than that of logic proper.

5. Love as a key notion in Hegel's early thought

It will be helpful in this connection to glance at a fragment dating from 1797–8 which foreshadows some of the central concepts of Hegelianism still more clearly. The subject of this fragment is again love, but the treatment, as will be seen, is broader than in 'The Spirit of Christianity'.

The piece begins, obscurely, with an attempt to characterize the attitude of men who are united in having accepted subjection to a distant God or universal law: sharp distinction and opposition, not only between themselves and their master but also between themselves and the world, are the order of the day in such circumstances. With this situation Hegel contrasts the relationship of love, for which opposition is at most provisional. I will quote at length the passage in which this idea gets its fullest development:[1]

> True union, or love proper, exists only between living beings who are alike in power and thus in one another's eyes living beings from every point of view; in no respect is either dead for the other. This genuine love excludes all oppositions. It is not the understanding, whose relations always leave the manifold of related terms as a manifold and whose unity is always a unity of opposites. It is not reason[2] either, because reason sharply opposes its determining power to what is determined. Love neither restricts nor is restricted; it is not finite at all. It is a feeling, yet not a single feeling. A single feeling is only a part and not the whole of life;

1. Knox, 304–5; Nohl, 379.   2. i.e. Kant's practical reason.

the life present in a single feeling dissolves its barriers and drives on till it disperses itself in the manifold of feelings with a view to finding itself in the entirety of this manifold. This whole life is not contained in love in the same way as it is in this sum of many particular and isolated feelings; in love, life is present as a duplicate of itself and as a single and unified self. Here life has run through the circle of development from an immature to a completely mature unity: when the unity was immature, there still stood over against it the world and the possibility of a cleavage between itself and the world; as development proceeded, reflection produced more and more oppositions (unified by satisfied impulses) until it set the whole of man's life in opposition; finally, love completely destroys objectivity and thereby annuls and transcends reflection, deprives man's opposite of all foreign character, and discovers life itself without any further defect. In love the separate does still remain, but as something united and no longer as something separate. Life senses life.

Love here, I suggest, is not simply a moral desideratum; it is serving as the model for a relationship which is satisfactory to thought as well. It is not just that we are called on to create the harmonious conditions of which Hegel here speaks; we are also to take what we see to be true of love at its best—its being, in later language, a true unity in diversity—and use it as a clue to the nature of things. To adopt anything short of this—for example, to rest content with the concepts of the reflective understanding with its hard-and-fast oppositions and distinctions—is evidently to fail to do justice to what we know to be true of living experience. In love, as Hegel puts it, life is present 'as a duplicate of itself', or to put it in another way which recalls a passage quoted earlier, love is a sort of analogon of reason, of the reason, that is to say, which Hegel was to distinguish from understanding and the concept of which he had not yet clearly grasped.[1]

---

1. See note on p. 139 above.

6. *Hegel on the inadequacies of religious language*

This last point deserves to be emphasized. For though love at this stage of Hegel's thinking played something of the part which speculative reason was subsequently to do, there are none the less important differences between the two. Bradley, after quoting from *The Phoenix and the Turtle* ('how true a twain/Seemeth this concordant one'), asserts boldly[1] that 'philosophy does not reach its end till the "reason of reason" is adequate to the "reason of love" '. Hegel in his mature years would certainly have agreed with this: the whole object of the Hegelian logic was to show not only that this was philosophy's ideal but also how it could be accomplished. In the late 1790s he was apparently less optimistic. He might well have allowed that the condition stated would have to be fulfilled if philosophy were to reach its end; but from this he drew the conclusion not that it must, but that it could not, do so. Much as Bradley himself argued in *Appearance and Reality* that no conceptual scheme could do justice to what we evidently knew to be the nature of the real, so was Hegel at this stage despondent about the prospects of philosophy. If the Absolute could be reached at all, it could be reached not by philosophy but by, or in, religion.

To clarify these points I must return first to 'The Spirit of Christianity'. I said above that Hegel's interests in the opening sections of this work were predominantly practical, but this is by no means true of the essay as a whole. Religion, not morals, was the main subject of his enquiry, and religion involves assertion as well as action. We must now glance at Hegel's views on the difficult problem of the form of religious statements.

What religion has to do on its propositional side is to express the infinite or, as Hegel alternatively puts it,[2] 'to conceive of pure life'. But this immediately raises difficulties. To speak of pure spirit in the terms of everyday language or 'reflection' is to objectify it and thus turn it into something different from what it is; it is to represent as divided what we know to be unitary. Hegel's conclusion that it is 'only in inspired terms that the divine can be spoken of'[3] (the

1. *Ethical Studies*, 2nd edition, p. 186, note.
2. Knox, 254; Nohl, 302.   3. Knox, 255; Nohl, 305.

German is 'nur in Begeisterung') evidently follows. But if we turn to the scriptures for examples of this sort of language we find, in the first place, that much of the phraseology used is, thanks to the Jewish heritage, intolerably harsh and materialistic: expressions like 'the kingdom of heaven', 'I am the door' and so on have implications altogether inappropriate to the subject.

The beginning of the gospel according to St. John appears to offer something better, since the sentences 'In the beginning was the Logos. The Logos was with God, and God was the Logos. In him was life' have, in Hegel's view,[1] 'only the deceptive semblance of judgments'. Their predicates, he explains, 'are not concepts, not universals like those necessarily contained in judgments expressing reflection. On the contrary, the predicates are themselves once more something bei.1g and living'. He immediately adds, however, that 'even this simple form of reflection is not adapted to the spiritual expression of spirit' and warns us that our understanding of what is said here depends on the amount of spiritual experience we ourselves bring to bear. 'Nowhere is it less possible to learn, to assimilate passively, because everything expressed about the divine in the language of reflection is eo ipso contradictory; and the passive spiritless assimilation of such an expression not only leaves the deeper spirit empty but also distracts the intellect which assimilates it and for which it is a contradiction'.[2] It is not surprising that, after a careful discussion of how the opening verses are to be taken, Hegel concludes that 'however sublime the idea of God may be made here', the expression is not satisfactory: where a 'living connection' is in question, 'ties between the related terms can be expressed only in mystical phraseology'.[3]

This is obviously the end of any hope for a true speculative philosophy. To complete this account of Hegel's early philosophical development I should like to refer to one more passage where he explicitly draws that conclusion, the first of the two pieces which make up what Nohl called the 'Fragment of a System' of 1800. The general subject of discussion is the concept of life, which Hegel takes up at three different levels.

First, he seems to be analysing the common-sense notion of an

1. Knox, 256; Nohl, 306.   2. Knox, 256; Nohl, 306.
3. 'Nur mystisch besprochen werden kann', Knox, 259; Nohl, 308.

individual human being living in distinction from other similar human beings; the argument, which is not clear, tries to establish that there is something abstract in this notion, that it is the product of 'reflection' which 'crystallizes' the infinite multiplicity of living beings 'into stable, subsistent and fixed points'.[1]

Next Hegel considers the idea of Nature, conceived organically in the manner which his friend Schelling was making fashionable. Nature so understood was thought to unite oneness and diversity, to be a single system differentiating itself as a multiplicity of individuals; Hegel suggests respectfully that the unity and diversity are not really shown to be there, but are imposed by reflection from the outside.

Dissatisfaction with this state of affairs, he argues,[2] leads to a third way of taking the concept of infinite life, namely as God:

> We may call infinite life a spirit in contrast with the abstract multiplicity, for spirit is the living unity of the manifold if it is contrasted with the manifold as spirit's configuration and not as a mere dead multiplicity; contrasted with the latter, spirit would be nothing but a bare unity which is called law and is something purely conceptual and not a living being. The spirit is an animating law in union with the manifold which is then itself animated. When man takes this animated manifold as a multiplicity of many individuals, yet as connected with the animating spirit, then these single lives become organs, and the infinite whole becomes an infinite totality of life. When he takes the infinite life as the spirit of the whole and at the same time as outside himself (since he himself is restricted), and when he puts himself at the same time outside his restricted self in rising toward the living being and intimately uniting himself with him, then he worships God.

Like the organic conception of Nature, these ideas were in the air at the time and were looked on with sympathy by Hegel; but he could not quite bring himself to accept them all the same. To say that God is living spirit, he points out shrewdly, you have to have

1. Knox, 310; Nohl, 346.   2. Knox, 311–12; Nohl, 347.

the idea of that which is not alive; to say he unites union and opposition (which might be a counter to the above move) you have to have the idea of what is not so united, of 'non-union', as Hegel calls it. 'In other words, every expression whatsoever is a product of reflection, and therefore it is possible to demonstrate in the case of every expression that, when reflection propounds it, another expression, not propounded, is excluded. Reflection is thus driven on and on without rest.'[1] What we have to recognize is that 'what has been called a union of synthesis and antithesis is not something propounded by the understanding or by reflection but has a character of its own, namely that of being a reality beyond all reflection'.[2] And this conclusion amounts in effect to saying that philosophy must yield pride of place to religion; it cannot be constructive, only negative. 'Philosophy has to disclose the finiteness in all finite things and require their integration by means of reason. In particular, it has to recognize the illusions generated by its own infinite and thus place the true infinite outside its confines.'[3]

7. *Discussion of Hegel's case*

It may seem odd to end a summary of Hegel's early philosophical thinking on a note of this kind, so evidently at variance with his later views. It is possible that we are misled by the survival of only two sheets from his 1800 manuscript and interpret these more negatively than we should if we could see them in context; perhaps in the missing portion there was some attempt to show how philosophy could after all become positive and comprehend the 'reality beyond all reflection'. At all events we find Hegel writing to Schelling, about the time he completed this particular manuscript, to say that he found he had to transform his youthful ideal into the form of reflection, into a system, with which he was then busy;[4] and soon after he went to Jena to teach philosophy in 1801 he was actually in possession of a system, or a substantial part of one. The important thing

1. Knox, 312; Nohl, 348.   2. ibid.
3. Knox, 313; Nohl, 348.
4. *Briefe von und an Hegel*, ed. J. Hoffmeister, I, 59 (2 November 1800).

for our purposes is that the main sources of that system are to be found in the material we have analysed.

If we proceed now to consider what there is to be said about the general subject on the evidence of this single case, the first point which stands out is that here at least we have to do with a metaphysical theory whose origins are not to be found in logic of any sort, good or bad. Hegel's initial intellectual preoccupations were with the nature and history of religion, a subject to which he was drawn because of the bearing he thought it evidently had on the practical problems of his own time. Acutely conscious of what has been picturesquely called the divided soul of modern man, and profoundly unhappy in the flat and fragmented society in which he lived, he sought at once for a satisfactory diagnosis of the situation and for a remedy for it. His studies in the religious and moral history of the Greeks, Jews and early Christians were perhaps undertaken in the first place to find out what in fact occurred, but in carrying out this seemingly academic task Hegel's thoughts were never far from the conditions of contemporary Germany. Like many historians, Hegel sought to assess as well as to describe; he was concerned to weigh the achievements of the ancients, and in so doing to pass judgment on their successors.

Similarly, when he came to expound the moral ideal of Jesus and the doctrine of a morality of love his interest was not exclusively, or even primarily, descriptive: the object was to say what would be truly satisfactory from the moral point of view, not merely to analyse a view which had actually been held. Admittedly Hegel directed the main weight of his attack here on the concepts of Kant's ethical system, which professed to be nothing but an explication of the moral thinking of ordinary men and to that extent to confine itself to reporting fact. But the ground on which the attack was mounted was much more that Kant's theory gave a morally unacceptable account of the moral life than that it misreported what the plain man believed.

It was thus in the course of producing a tolerable scheme of ideas for dealing with moral phenomena that Hegel first devised his own characteristic way of thinking. And the criteria he used in deciding for or against such a scheme were twofold: on the one hand intellectual coherence, on the other what may be called moral acceptability.

Now it might well be argued that if this is a correct account of the matter the consequences are not very flattering for Hegel. For on this view Hegel must, it would seem, be taken as first having laid down that society ought to be penetrated by spirit along the lines sketched above, and then concluded that the world as a whole is nothing but the self-expression of spirit. There would be a move here from what is morally satisfactory and ought to be to what is intellectually satisfactory and must be thought to be, a move which even Hegel's logical ingenuity could scarcely make respectable. Certainly his later assurance, in the preface to the *Philosophy of Right*, that philosophy has nothing to say about what ought to be, only about what is, would not suffice to do the trick.

But the matter is scarcely as simple as this objection suggests. For one thing, the sharp opposition here drawn between what ought to be and what must be thought to be would not be at all to Hegel's liking. He would certainly have rejected the view that the activity of deciding on the proper conditions of social or personal life constituted, or belonged to, a self-contained department of life or language game, on very much the same grounds as were advanced in the last chapter. To take up a moral attitude, in his opinion, was among other things to make a theoretical commitment: in Kant's case, for example, it involved the belief, explicitly set out in Kant's doctrine of phenomena and noumena, that man is a creature with a dual nature. One reason why Hegel rejected Kant's ethics was that he thought they were built on a theoretical presupposition, about the relationship of the inclinations and practical reason, which was false.

In his criticism of Jewish beliefs, again, it is clear that Hegel was not merely objecting on moral grounds to an approach to conduct which he considered slavish and lifeless. The centre of his objection was clearly practical, yet the thought that the underlying conceptual scheme was not as it should be from the theoretical point of view was never far from his mind. This comes out in Hegel's tendency, illustrated repeatedly in the essays under consideration, to move from moral to metaphysical language without any thought of incongruity, and to present the final position in terms drawn from the vocabulary of logic: witness, for example, his transition from the master/slave antithesis to that of (abstract) universal and particular.

Nor is Abraham at the beginning of 'The Spirit of Christianity' meant to illustrate a purely moral attitude. True, he is denounced as loveless and hateful, but that is not the end of the matter, for Hegel is clearly suggesting that in trying to preserve his own integrity by total withdrawal from the world he is attempting something which is theoretically impossible. Abraham, in fact, represents a metaphysical as well as a moral position; he should be compared in this respect with Antoine Roquentin in Sartre's novel *La Nausée*.

I said above that Hegel's criteria for a tolerable way of thinking about the moral world were intellectual coherence and moral acceptability. It emerges from the last two paragraphs that the first of these is less innocent than it sounds, for Hegel is insisting not only that a scheme of moral ideas be free from formal contradiction, but further that the presuppositions on which it rests be capable of sustaining critical examination. He would certainly have rejected many such schemes which appear from the formal point of view to be perfectly in order, e.g. hedonistic utilitarianism, which rested in his view on an impossible conception of pleasure.[1] And whatever value we attach to his comments on the coherence of particular ways of thinking about conduct, there seems no doubt that the move from morals so conceived to metaphysics is altogether less extravagant than it originally appeared to be.

But this is not all. I have spoken so far as if Hegel's sole ground for thinking that reality is the self-expression of spirit was that we must employ this notion to make sense of the moral world. Now in the first place it is not strictly true that Hegel in his early writings is at any point exclusively concerned with morals. He discourses on conduct at length, but it is conduct set in a religious context which really claims his attention. To be fair to him we must accordingly take account of his views on religion, and think of him as speaking, not just of what it is to act rightly or conscientiously, but of what it is to do this against a background of religious beliefs. And that this contention is important we can see when we reflect that Hegel at this stage would have rejected any attempt to think of religion as purely a matter of practice. To accept Christianity, for him, was not merely a matter of letting your life be guided by Christian precepts;

1. Compare the arguments used by Bradley against Mill in his essay 'Pleasure for pleasure's sake' in *Ethical Studies*.

it was further to be committed intellectually to the main tenets of Christian theology.

It is true that Hegel began his reflection on these matters with a strong antipathy to formal theology, and again that he maintained throughout these formative years an attitude to religious orthodoxy which was critical where not positively hostile. But he soon abandoned his early advocacy of a religion of all good men free of doctrine and dogma, and he would certainly not have seen any inconsistency in rejecting official Christianity whilst insisting that at the centre of the Christian gospel there were affirmations which were profoundly true. The really striking thing about the works with which we have been concerned, and particularly about 'The Spirit of Christianity', is the way in which Hegel sets out there from the assumption that what the Christian is trying to express, the doctrine of the primacy of spirit, is self-evidently correct, and that the problem is not so much to defend as to articulate it.[1] Nor is his belief at the end of the period that it was incapable of formal articulation evidence that he entertained doubts about the validity of this central insight. If philosophy could not 'think' the reality which lay beyond all reflection, the proper conclusion to draw was so much the worse for philosophy.

Hegel's type of philosophy has been denounced as resting on mysticism, and again as deliberately obscurantist, but there seems no adequate ground for convicting him of these defects. He differs from other philosophers not in seeking refuge in mysticism but in taking it seriously:[2] the very fact that there is such a thing as religious language seems to him a datum which cannot be ignored, and he builds much of his philosophy around this datum. It was not the only positive source of his ideas, as we can see from the frequent mention he makes of the notion of life, but it was all the same an important source. To describe Hegelianism as secularized theology is not extravagant, however unfavourable the impression Hegel has made on some religious men.

1. It may be worth mentioning in this connection that Hegel was originally a divinity student, intending to be a pastor in the Lutheran Church.
2. In his lectures on the history of philosophy Hegel gave Boehme more space than Leibniz, and much more than Hume.

As for the other charge, Hegel is often obscure, but that is not the same as being obscurantist. He is obscure·thanks to his curious predilection for putting concrete insights in highly abstract terms, preferably taken from the language of logic; the result of this is that his real thought is more often disguised than not. This defect is one which grew on him: it is present, but not prominent, in the early writings, more obvious, though still not quite unmitigated, in the *Phenomenology*, and at its worst in the larger *Logic* and the *Encyclopaedia*, where Hegel's ideas are supposed to find definitive expression. An innocent reader can go through these last-named works, or large parts of them, like one in a dream, conscious that a highly complicated game is being played, aware perhaps of some of the rules which govern the moves, yet failing all the time to grasp what the whole performance is intended to signify. The impression that there is nothing there but a species of logical jugglery is readily formed. Attention to the essays with which we have been concerned in this chapter should do something to remove that impression, for they show how, despite first appearances, Hegel was really preoccupied with concrete rather than abstract questions, and demonstrate that the ideas which move in the rarefied atmosphere of the mature system were originally conceived a good deal nearer to earth.

We may find Hegel's metaphysics implausible because we can see little or nothing in his basic insight, or we may think that his attempt to apply this basic insight and produce a connected account of experience is unsuccessful. But we cannot accuse him with any show of truth of spinning his whole system out of mere ideas. To take him as a logician pure and simple is not only to misunderstand the Hegelian conception of logic; it is to be content with the barest superficialities, instead of penetrating behind them to the thought they are meant to express.[1]

1. In this account of the origins of Hegelianism I have naturally concentrated on the positive sources of the system. But it should be added that one powerful feature which commends his thought is the incisiveness of his criticism of what he called the philosophers of the Understanding, the analytic thinkers of his day. Many of the strictures brought by modern philosophers against the philosophical practice of working with hard-and-fast distinctions and sharp antitheses were already anticipated by Hegel. So if Wittgenstein on games is not quite Hegel on the concrete universal, there is at any rate a family resemblance between the two.

10

Metaphysical Assertion and Metaphysical Argument

IN THIS chapter I shall be concerned, in the first place, to say more about the specific character of metaphysical pronouncements, a subject which has already been touched on in the concluding pages of Chapter 5 (pp. 77 ff. above). I shall try in particular to bring out and elaborate the connection there hinted at between taking up a metaphysical position and having a view on where to draw the line between sense and nonsense; I shall also indicate where, in my view, the suggestive treatment of these topics by Collingwood succeeds and where it fails. I shall then go on, in the light of my conclusions in the first part of the chapter, to say something of the types of argument to which metaphysicians can make appeal in support of their positions. All this will be a preliminary to discussion of the all-important question of truth and falsity in metaphysics, which will form the subject of the next chapter.

1. *Formal, material, categorial sense and nonsense*

A good point from which to start a discussion of the nature of metaphysical assertions is the Positivist dogma that there are only two kinds of significant proposition: those which, in Hume's terminology, express relations of ideas and those which inform us about matter of fact and existence. My first task now will be to demonstrate that this analysis overlooks a further class of statements whose significance is obvious and whose relevance to metaphysics can, I believe, be made apparent. But instead of approaching this task directly I shall proceed to consider a counterpart of the Positivist dogma. I refer to the commonly accepted view that there are two and only two species of absurdity or nonsense, material and formal. A man falls into material absurdity, or talks nonsense in a material sense, if he maintains something which patently conflicts with the well-attested findings of some recognized discipline, or ignores obvious facts which any reasonable person would acknowledge. Formal absurdity is perpetrated, or formal nonsense talked, when someone says something which violates the rules of formal logic; for instance when he says something corresponding to the logical formula $p \& \sim p$. It is widely believed that, once the relatively unimportant case of grammatical nonsense has been set aside, the dichotomy of material and formal is here exhaustive. But that this is false can be shown without any difficulty. Consider the following examples:[1]

1. I am being driven by a friend in a motor-car when, without warning, the engine stops and the car comes to a standstill. I ask my friend what has happened: he replies that the car has stopped for no reason at all. I laugh politely at what I take to be his joke and wait for an explanation or for some activity on my friend's part to discover what has gone wrong; he remains in his seat and neither says nor does anything more. Trying not to appear rude, I presently ask my friend whether he knows much about motor-cars, the implication being that his failure to look for the cause of the breakdown must be explained by his just not knowing how to set about the job. He takes my point at once and tells me that it is not a question of ignorance or knowledge; there just was no reason for the stoppage. Puzzled, I ask him if he means that it was a miracle, brought about by the intervention of what eighteenth-century writers called a 'particular Providence'. Being philosophically sophisticated, he replies that to explain something as being due to an act of God is to give a reason, though not a natural reason, whereas what he said was that there was no reason for what occurred. At this point I lose my temper and tell him not to talk nonsense, for (I say) 'Things just don't happen for no reason at all'.

1. What follows (to the end of the section) is taken, with minor alterations, from my article 'Categories', first printed in *Kantstudien* (1953–4), pp. 274–8.

2. A calls on B at an awkward moment when B has dropped his collar-stud and cannot find it. 'I had it in my hand a moment ago,' he tells his friend, 'so it can't be far off.' The search goes on for some time without success, until A suddenly asks B what makes him think the stud is there to be found. Controlling himself, B explains that he had the stud in his hand and was trying to do up his collar when it slipped from his fingers; that there are no holes in the floor; that the windows of the room are unusually high; and that if the stud had come to pieces he must certainly have come across some bit of it after looking for so long. 'Ah,' says A, 'but have you considered the possibility that it may have vanished without trace?' 'Vanished without trace?' asks B; 'do you mean turned into gaseous form, gone off like a puff of smoke or something of that sort? Collar-studs don't do things like that.' 'No, that isn't what I mean,' A assures him gravely; 'I mean literally vanished without trace, passed clean out of existence.' Words fail B at this point, but it is clear from the look he gives his friend that he takes him either to be making an ill-timed joke or to be talking downright nonsense, a proceeding which only his being a philosopher will excuse.

What sort of nonsense is talked by someone who asserts seriously that events sometimes happen for no reason at all or that things sometimes vanish without trace, passing clean out of existence?

Is it *formal* nonsense as defined above? There is a strong temptation for philosophers to say that it is, for the contradictories of the statements in question are often formulated in terms of necessity ('There *must* always be a reason for whatever occurs', 'Things *cannot* vanish without trace'), and it is very common to identify necessary with analytic statements. Some philosophers, indeed, make the identification a matter of definition; they hold that the only statements entitled to the description 'necessary' are those whose truth depends on logical considerations. Of this dogma no more need be said now than that the statements with which we are concerned seem *prima facie* to count against it, for there is nothing logically impossible in the notion of an event happening for no reason at all or of a thing vanishing without trace and passing clean out of existence. Of course we could, if we chose, make it a matter of definition that nothing should be *called* an event unless we believed it happened for a reason, and similarly in the other case; but it is plain that this would not solve the problem. There is an important difference between saying 'There are no events which happen for no reason at all' and saying 'There are no "events" which happen for no reason at all'.

Is then to make the statements in question to talk nonsense in the *material* sense? To many philosophers this would seem the only possible thing to say, once the thesis that it was formal nonsense had been considered and rejected. But this alternative seems no more satisfactory than the other. A man talks nonsense in the material sense, as was explained above, if he fails to take account, or asserts the contradictory, of some obvious and well-attested fact, or of some well-established piece of theory; as for example if I say that you can put a kettle on the gas stove, light the gas and find after ten minutes that the water has not changed its temperature. But in the examples given neither mistakes of fact nor mistakes of theory entered into the question. When my friend asserted that the car had stopped for no reason at all he was not putting forward an empirical hypothesis to the effect that this or that suggested explanation was false; he was asserting bluntly that there just was no explanation. It is true that if somebody said this sort of thing in real life he would be taken as asserting either that he did not know the explanation or that none of the obvious explanations of this kind of happening would fit; but this is only because we should be unwilling to take him at his word. It would not be flattering to the man to suppose that he was talking such nonsense.

This point can perhaps be made clearer if we turn our attention to the other example about a thing vanishing without trace. Of course there is a sense in which we regard it as perfectly sensible to say of something that it vanished without trace. Buildings or features of the landscape can be obliterated without trace by a hurricane or a nuclear explosion; if fortunately few of us have personal experience of events of this sort, we know perfectly well that they occur. But of course we also know that the expression 'vanished without trace' is used with certain unspoken reservations on these occasions. When the team of scientists responsible for an atomic test reports to its government that all the buildings on the island where the test took place vanished without trace, it is not meant that there is no answer to the question

'What became of them?'. They along with many other solid-looking objects were vaporized by the heat of the explosion and scattered to the four winds. But buildings which vaporize and scatter to the four winds do not vanish without trace in an unqualified sense of those words; they merely leave no trace of themselves on the spot where they stood. What A suggested to B in my example was that the collar-stud might have vanished without trace in an unqualified sense: that particular bit of matter might have gone clean out of existence, leaving no trace of itself in solid, liquid or gaseous form. If that had happened it would not make sense to ask the question what became of it, and this is what gives interest to the example for our purposes.

Hume in his essay on miracles mentions the case of an 'Indian' prince who refused to believe that water turned into ice in conditions of great cold.[1] The position of someone who is incredulous about the report that solid buildings disappeared without trace when a nuclear device was exploded is similar to that of this prince. Both have to learn that the boundaries of empirical possibility are not to be measured by any particular man's stock of empirical knowledge. Surprising as it may be, water turns into a solid in one set of circumstances and buildings vaporize in another. But however odd these events may seem to the unsophisticated, it would be even odder if water or buildings were to vanish without trace, in the sense of being not transmuted but annihilated. It would, in fact, be another species of oddity altogether.

Doubts about the applicability on specific occasions of the questions 'What was the reason for this?' and 'What became of that?' are not material doubts in the sense in which a doubt whether water will solidify if cooled is material. It is not facts or supposed facts which are challenged by such a doubt, but rather what I must call the framework of facts. The statements that nothing happens except for a reason and that nothing vanishes without trace in the unqualified sense of the phrase are, with the concepts which underlie them, of a higher logical order than are empirical statements and concepts; they provide a scaffolding, or constitute a pre-existing mould, inside which we build up or present our empirical knowledge. That is why any attempt to question them is felt to be more serious than an

1. *Enquiry*, pp. 113–14, ed. Selby-Bigge.

attempt to question even a widely accepted empirical statement. To discover that what we had believed to be materially true is false may come as a profound shock; but the shock is nothing like so great as would be that of discovering that there were events which occurred for no reason or things which went clean out of existence.

An alternative way of expressing what has just been said is this. If we were asked to write down as full a list as possible of true empirical statements, we should not (or ought not to) include the statements that nothing happens except for a reason and that nothing vanishes without trace in the sense of passing clean out of existence. These statements are rather presuppositions of empirical truths than empirical truths themselves. What is more (and this point is crucial) they are presuppositions of a very unusual kind. As Collingwood made clear,[1] every question has presuppositions in so far as asking the question implies that something is true. Thus if I ask what is the name of the French Prime Minister I imply that someone is French Prime Minister. Most implications of this sort can be made the subject of further enquiry: we can ask e.g. whether it is in fact true that there is a Prime Minister of France. Presuppositions of this sort, which are themselves answers to further questions, are called by Collingwood 'relative presuppositions'. The distinguishing mark of such presuppositions as that which underlay my question to my friend when the motor-car broke down, that there must be a reason for whatever happens, is that we cannot sensibly make them the subject of further questioning. There is no process of consulting fact which will establish them, in the way in which such a process is relevant to the question whether France has a Prime Minister. Hence, as Collingwood put it, they are 'absolute', not 'relative', presuppositions.

We need some convenient name for the class of statements of which the two statements in my examples are instances. Following Kant, I propose to call them 'categorial principles' and the concepts which underlie them 'categories'. And I shall say that the man who disregards or questions categorial principles is talking categorial nonsense.

---

1. In his *Essay on Metaphysics*, and also in his *Autobiography*.

2. *Categorial principles and metaphysics*

To recognize the existence of a distinct class of categorial principles is already to blunt the weapon which Professor Nowell-Smith has aptly named Hume's Fork, the instrument Hume relied on in arguing that books of divinity and school metaphysics should be consigned to the flames. But it is not enough in itself to vindicate the respectability of metaphysics, if only because the connection between metaphysics and categorial principles remains to be elucidated. On this point Collingwood had a simple, if somewhat surprising, view: he held that the business of metaphysicians was to discover and make explicit absolute presuppositions. It seemed to Collingwood not only that there are principles which are presupposed absolutely, but further that there must be, for statements are made in response to questions, spoken or unspoken, and all questioning proceeds on presuppositions, not all of which can become the subject of further enquiry. At any particular time there will accordingly be presuppositions which are treated as absolute. But relatively few people are aware of what they are presupposing in this way, and still fewer know that the ultimate presuppositions of their age are not necessarily identical with those of previous ages. A special activity of analysis is required to make absolute presuppositions explicit, and it is on this activity, Collingwood assures us, that metaphysicians have always been engaged.

Collingwood was driven to this paradoxical identification of metaphysics with history of a certain kind by observing that absolute presuppositions cannot be said to be true or false. If they are not true or false, he seems to have argued, there can be no question of choosing rationally between alternative sets of them. So metaphysics cannot consist in the advocacy of what is regarded as *the* correct set of first principles; if it is to be a rational activity, it must eschew the question what *should* be presupposed, and confine itself to elucidating what *is* or *has been* presupposed.

The first difficulty in this account is to square it with actual metaphysical practice. Collingwood himself argued that it applied clearly to the case of Kant, whose *Critique of Pure Reason* contrived to make explicit the ultimate assumptions which underlay Newtonian science. But Kant certainly intended to do more than this: he thought he could justify Newton, not merely expound him. The aim of the Analytic of Principles was to uncover necessary conditions to which all thinking about objects must conform, and the standpoint Kant took up there was certainly not that of a mere spectator. Kant's professions at least would not square with Collingwood's theory.

Collingwood could have appealed for support to Hegel with more plausibility, since Hegel notoriously held that Plato's *Republic* was not a Utopia, but a reflection of current political thought and practice. Philosophy, in the famous epigram in the preface to the *Philosophy of Right*, paints its grey on grey only when a form of life has grown old; the owl of Minerva takes to flight only at twilight. But however appropriate this may be for Hegel's ethics and politics, it is hard to take it seriously as an account of his logic and metaphysics. The *Phenomenology of Spirit*, which purports to offer an introduction to Hegel's system, may indeed be seen as primarily a document of its time, but the same could hardly be claimed for the *Science of Logic*, which professes to put forward a series of timeless truths. Nor for that matter is it in the least plausible to represent Hegel as merely describing a number of attitudes to the world in that work; his standpoint throughout is critical. He urges a distinctive point of view on his readers, and presents its alternatives as radically incoherent rather than merely outmoded. Whatever his theory, his philosophical practice scarcely corresponds to Collingwood's prescription. But in this there is nothing peculiar, for it is hard to think of any metaphysician who has simply been engaged in making ultimate presuppositions explicit. There is a sense in which metaphysicians do build on presuppositions, as Aristotle perhaps built on the assumptions of biological science and as materialists build on those of physics. But what they do with the principles in question in cases like these is certainly more than just to point them out.

There is a second difficulty in Collingwood's theory which is of more interest for our present purposes. The doctrine of absolute presuppositions is taken by him as carrying with it the legitimization of metaphysics, since metaphysics in his view consists in stating what is absolutely presupposed. But a critic of metaphysics, whilst admitting that there are principles which function as absolute presuppositions, might argue that it is one thing to act on such a pre-supposition, and another to advocate a metaphysical point of view. The distinguishing mark of the latter, as we have already made clear, is its overall character: a metaphysician approaches experience of any kind with the same general assumptions, claiming that the same principles apply to every aspect of the word. But a man could accept such a principle as beyond question and still give it a restricted application; and indeed there is every reason to think that men constantly do just this. There are many distinguished scientists who would regard it as unthinkable that anything could happen in their laboratories which was not to be explained in natural terms, but who nevertheless abandon this attitude when they go to church, finding no difficulty there in assenting to the Virgin Birth or the Resurrection. To say that such men are untrue to their own scientific principles is unfair, for, as they would hasten to point out themselves, the assumptions on which they proceed as scientists were never intended by them to be valid outside the field of science. That one thing should be true in this field and another outside it does not strike them as a paradox, however much others may think that it should. They keep their science and their religion in watertight compartments, and in so far as they do act on absolute presuppositions without committing themselves to the metaphysics of materialism.

What this comes to is that recognition of the existence and func-tioning of categorial principles is compatible with metaphysical neutralism, an attitude which I have previously suggested is in-coherent but which is all the same widely taken up. Contrary to what may at first appear, you do not discover a man's metaphysics when you find out the principles he is prepared to accept without question. The fact remains, even so, that such principles often are good evidence of metaphysical beliefs, for they are often put to metaphysical use.

This happens in the case of the materialist, as was previously explained, at the point where the principle that nothing occurs which cannot be accounted for in natural terms ceases to function merely as an absolute presupposition underlying a restricted set of questions, namely those asked by natural scientists in the course of their scientific enquiries, and is extended to cover questions of any sort, including those asked in the fields of morals and religion. The materialist, like his fellow metaphysicians, wants a single interpretative scheme; he is not willing to allow talk of miracles or the grace of God to make any serious sense. Nor would he accept the compromise proffered by the tender-minded according to which science and religion can peacefully coexist, each being allowed to pursue its activities where it will: his thesis is that truth can be arrived at only by scientific means. Such a view does not, of course, dispute the plain facts that religion and morals are important parts of human life, nor need its exponents adopt the more technical philosophical thesis that religious and moral discourse can be reduced to scientific discourse without loss of meaning. What is being urged is rather that, if you want to make sense of these activities, you must do so inside a scheme which is fundamentally scientific, and for whose exponents it is axiomatic that understanding can be had only in natural terms. On this point the mind of a materialist is fully made up; he regards the suggestion that there are more things in heaven and earth than are dreamt of in his philosophy as fantastic or absurd.

We have had occasion earlier to raise the question to what extent materialism can be taken as typical of metaphysics. If materialism is understood in the way we are taking it here, as the advocacy of an overall interpretative scheme, it is obvious that there are metaphysical systems which are on the face of it very different. Setting out to tell us what the world is really like, they tend to take the form of ontologies, doctrines of 'what there is' or enumerations of the kinds of substance to which things ultimately happen.[1] It looks here as if the metaphysician must necessarily be a rival to mere empirical enquirers; it looks again as if he must assert the existence of entities whose presence cannot be discovered by empirical means or established by straightforward empirical arguments.

Yet we saw reason, in our previous discussion, to think that many other metaphysical systems besides materialism could be plausibly presented as each embodying a theory of first principles, to use a phrase which has long been prominent in the literature of the subject. They can be seen, that is to say, as a series of attempts to tell us how to get the different aspects of our experience into perspective. And

1. Some metaphysical theories of this kind dispense with the conception of substance, on the ground that processes are ultimate, so the above explanation of 'ontology' must be taken as only approximate.

though it is characteristic of such attempts to announce that all sorts of unfamiliar entities exist (even materialism tells us that nothing is ultimately there except matter), it is perhaps a mistake to treat such announcements as intended to convey information. To say that spirit alone is real, or that in the end everything is swallowed up in the Absolute, is evidently not to imply that chairs and tables are imaginary, or individual things fictitious; it is to suggest that we must think of the world in a certain way if we are to understand it. The Absolute is not the sort of thing one could meet with, anyway; it is not a constituent of the world, familiar or unfamiliar. And the same perhaps goes for God as he figures in metaphysical theories, if not for the God of religion. Individual metaphysicians have not always appreciated these points: as we saw, Plato was committed by his theory of knowledge to the view that Forms are actual existents,[1] though they did not exist in space and time, whilst for Aquinas the search for metaphysical understanding was too closely bound up with religious practice for him to be willing to accept anything but an existential account of God. Yet if we remain at a level which is at once theoretical and rational we shall see the claims about existence made by metaphysicians as subordinate to their pretence to comprehend the scheme of things entire.

If all this is correct, there will lie at the centre of each metaphysical system a series of categorial principles, treated as having unrestricted validity. Metaphysicians urge such principles on us, on the plea that only by accepting them can we hope to arrive at a connected and coherent account of our experience as a whole. Now it might appear from this that metaphysics is not propositional at all, and thus that the answer to the question 'What is the logical character of metaphysical assertions?' is that there are none.

But this would evidently be to go too far. The fact is, of course, that no metaphysician is content to issue a set of injunctions and leave the matter at that: as well as urging us to see the world in a certain way he wants to show that it must be seen in this way. And to

---

1. In *Republic*, V, the 'lovers of sights and sounds' are accused of recognizing the existence of the many beautifuls but failing to recognize that of 'the beautiful itself'. The word νομίζω in this passage means 'take to exist', 'take to be the case', and τὰ τῶν πολλῶν νόμιμα (*Rep.* 479d) are what the many take to be the case (about the beautiful, etc.).

this end he not only has to bring counter-arguments against his rivals, but also to display liberal examples of the treatment he recommends, a process which involves him in much detailed description and interpretation. Much metaphysical argument consists in the adducing of facts to support or refute a theory. It is alleged that this or that feature of experience can only be understood if the underlying metaphysical attitude is accepted, or conversely that no sense can be made of it so long as that attitude is persisted with. Facts are mentioned as frequently in metaphysical as in legal disputes, and their role in the two is in some respects identical, in so far as they serve not to validate or invalidate principles, but to reveal in a less direct way their adequacy or inadequacy. A system of metaphysics which cannot get round facts which are at first sight awkward for its pretensions is like a system of law which cannot be applied. We may admire the architecture of the one or the other, but we cannot claim that it does the job for which it was designed.

It follows from this that a metaphysical treatise will be found to contain assertions of many kinds, including simple statements of fact, but that its central contentions will consist in, or be closely related to, a series of categorial principles. What Collingwood called the 'metaphysical rubric' takes the form of saying that *it is out of the question* or *absurd* to think so-and-so. For the materialist it is out of the question to think that there might be features of experience which could not be satisfactorily accounted for in natural terms; for Aristotle it was out of the question that things should not serve a purpose. To say that nothing happens except for a natural reason is seemingly to state a very general empirical fact. But the foregoing discussion should have shown that it functions rather as an ultimate presupposition, licensing the asking of a certain kind of question, to which it is hoped that experience will provide the answers. However wide of the mark Collingwood may have been in his final account of metaphysics, he made an enormous advance in recognizing the importance for metaphysics of presuppositions of this kind.

In the very first paragraph of this book I mentioned the claim that metaphysical pronouncements are in some way uniquely certain. It will be evident that the preceding argument lends only qualified support to this claim. In so far as commitment to a metaphysical position means commitment to a set of categorial principles, the metaphysician may be said to take his stand on something which is regarded as beyond question, for the suggestion that principles of this sort might not hold is treated by those who adhere to them as absurd. But the absurdity here in question is certainly not formal absurdity: there is no possibility of showing that those who advocate alternative sets of first principles are involved in self-contradiction. A man who maintains that things can happen for no reason at all may be accused of wanton love of paradox, but he can scarcely be convicted of logical inconsistency. Nor does there seem to be any ground for the view to which some metaphysicians have subscribed, that metaphysical truths are such that the very attempt to deny them involves their reaffirmation. The truth, if it is a truth, that everything can be explained satisfactorily in natural terms is certainly not reaffirmed in being denied, nor is its idealist rival that the only way to understand things is in terms of spirit. If there is anything compulsive about metaphysical principles (and certainly those who accept them are accustomed to think of them in this way), they are at least not logically compulsive. It would, indeed, be difficult to think of them as being really significant if they were.

One final point on this subject: what I have been describing as metaphysical principles should not be regarded as premises from which the metaphysician argues. Aristotle did not deduce conclusions from his principle that all things serve a purpose: he sought to apply it and let it govern his thought. It functioned in his thinking as a rule. Unfortunately there has been much confusion in the minds of metaphysicians about this matter, with consequent misapprehension of the proper nature of metaphysical argument. To this topic we must now turn.

3. *Proof and argument, principles and premises in metaphysics*

The great metaphysicians of the seventeenth century were obsessed with the idea of demonstrated knowledge. If metaphysics was to make good its claim to be queen of the sciences, it must be as closely argued as mathematics and present conclusions which were, if possible, still more ineluctable than those of Euclid. Hence the attempt, initiated by Descartes but carried out in detail only by

Spinoza, to present metaphysical thought in strict deductive form. Spinoza in his *Ethics* began by setting out a series of propositions which he described as definitions and axioms; these were such, he supposed, that they must be accepted as self-evidently true by anyone who fully understood what they involved. He then went on to offer what purported to be strict demonstrations of the main points of his philosophy, demonstrations which ostensibly made appeal only to what was granted in the definitions and axioms or to what had been previously proved on the basis of these. The questions what the world is truly like and how the wise man should behave in it were questions which for Spinoza could be answered with absolute certainty.

Descartes put his finger on the difficulty of this method of philosophizing when, in setting out his proofs of God's existence in the mathematical manner, he remarked that the trouble lay in establishing the initial premises of such a system.[1] Like Spinoza, Descartes himself thought that the ultimate test of the acceptability of such premises must lie in their clarity and distinctness, i.e. in their being patent to reason; but he showed more caution than his successor in specifying what was patent to reason, at least in his metaphysics. Moreover, he was troubled by a further consideration which does not seem to have worried Spinoza to the same extent. As a result of the sceptical arguments mentioned in an earlier chapter he had convinced himself that mathematical knowledge itself left something to be desired; its applicability to real situations was at least in theory open to doubt. A system of metaphysical knowledge must avoid this defect by starting from a premise which was at once a necessary truth, in the way mathematical truths are necessary, and a truth of fact. He found such a premise, as we all know, in the famous formula *cogito ergo sum*.

I have already argued (pp. 87 ff. above) that the *cogito* will not give Descartes the premise he desires. 'I exist' indeed follows from 'I think', and there is a sense in which 'I am not thinking' is self-refuting. But nothing significant can be deduced from these facts.[2]

1. Reply to Second Objections: Haldane and Ross, *Philosophical Works of Descartes*, II, 49–50.
2. Except perhaps that the word 'I', unlike other demonstratives and proper names, cannot be misused.

For in the first place it is not a truth of logic that I think: I must exist if I am to think, and I might not have existed. This becomes immediately clear if we substitute 'Walsh thinks' for 'I think'. And secondly, though I cannot use the word 'I' and not exist, the words 'I exist' do not, in the context of the Cartesian argument, convey any information. They *could* be used to make a meaningful claim (cf. what was said about 'I exist too' on pp. 88–9), but only if we abandon any pretence that they express a necessary truth. To put the matter shortly: in so far as 'I exist' is a necessary truth it says nothing, and in so far as it says something it is not a necessary truth.

The only move open to Cartesians in this situation is to argue that the *cogito* presents us with a proposition which is self-evidently true not in the formal but in a material sense, i.e. that it embodies, or issues in, a 'basic intuition'. Intuitions of this sort, alleged to be discerned by the eye of the mind, played a major part in the thinking of the great rationalists. But despite much effort they were not able to specify what distinguishes an acceptable from an unacceptable intuition in metaphysics: the criteria of clarity and distinctness were not themselves sufficiently clear and distinct. Nor indeed could they have been made so, except by turning the necessary truths on which the whole system was to rest into a series of idle tautologies.

The search for an ineluctable first premise for metaphysics was not peculiar to the seventeenth century. Plato in the *Republic* had spoken of an ἀνυπόθετος ἀρχή, an unhypothetical or unhypothesized first principle, as that from which the dialectician would make his start, unfortunately without indicating what form such a principle would take. Aristotle in the *Metaphysics* had sought to demonstrate that the laws of identity and contradiction, which he took as being truths of fact as well as laws of thought, were such that their validity was presupposed in any attempt to deny them. At a later stage the Idealists were to suggest that there was no rational alternative to their philosophy, since it followed from premises which had to be accepted if anything was to be accepted at all: as Bosanquet put it, it was a case of 'this or nothing'. Yet the unsatisfactoriness of this procedure, and of the accompanying attempts to argue that rival metaphysicians must be involved in self-contradiction, is sufficiently shown in the fact that these diverse parties appealed to it. Had mathematics been the true model for metaphysics, and had it really been possible to find a metaphysical premise which was compulsive in the way the *cogito* was intended to be, one system of metaphysics would long ago have been recognized as definitive. The fact that this has not happened is enough to show that it cannot.

Plato, Aristotle and their successors were quite right to speak of metaphysical principles, but they misunderstood their logical character. They saw them as ἀρχαί in the literal sense, i.e. as starting-points upon which other assertions were to be based, in a word as basic premises. We have argued above that what distinguishes a metaphysician from plain men on the one hand and his fellow practitioners on the other is not the premises he starts from but the principles of interpretation he brings to bear. There is no such thing as a special stock of knowledge accessible only to metaphysicians, nor is it the case that some metaphysicians have a grasp of fundamental truths of fact which are unaccountably lost sight of by others. We all confront the same world, but we differ in our ways of taking it.

The problem of establishing the validity of a system of metaphysics is that of establishing the validity of a set of principles of interpretation. It should be clear from our previous discussion that principles of this kind can be grounded neither deductively nor inductively. Absolute presuppositions can evidently not be deduced from further truths, or they would not be absolute; *a fortiori*, they cannot be deduced from supposedly basic truths of fact. But equally they cannot be established empirically, though experience may and does suggest them. Categorial principles are not read out of, but read into, experience; it is our refusal to give them up in the face of unfavourable evidence which differentiates them from highly general empirical laws. To suppose that they could be arrived at by a simple survey of the facts is once more to fail to understand the part they play in human thinking.

Metaphysics fundamentally is neither deductive like mathematics nor inductive like (elementary) natural science. But this is not to say that deductive and inductive argument have no place in the subject. Metaphysicians, like the rest of us, make constant use of deductive inference: they are constantly asserting that, p being the case, and p implying q which in turn implies r, we are logically committed to r, or arguing that, since q is false and p implies q, then p must be false also. Again, they make frequent use of analogical reasoning: they have an eye for likenesses of structure more acute than that of most of us and a tendency to extrapolate readily from partially discerned to overall patterns. And though no metaphysical position is open to direct empirical confutation, it remains true that serious metaphysicians are always sensitive to fact and vividly aware of the possibility that failure to do justice to it may render their whole theory unplausible.

Yet it may well be asked how all this can be true without our having to surrender any claim to scientific status which can be advanced on behalf of metaphysics. At an earlier stage of this book I spoke of the element of insight which seems to be involved in the work of comprehending a metaphysical theory: to say anything useful about such a theory one has to share the author's view of the world, and this quasi-imaginative activity is no less important than being able to follow his formal argument. In the more detailed discussions of the present chapter it has become clear that a metaphysical point of view is less subjective than this would suggest: imaginative insight may be part, but is certainly not the whole, of it. Yet the factor of unsupported assertion in metaphysics remains, even on this view, disturbingly high: to suggest that a man's metaphysics reflects his temperament rather than his comprehension of reality does not seem in these circumstances far-fetched. Unless we can meet this challenge we shall have to allow that the Positivist attack on metaphysics is ultimately successful: though not perhaps senseless in the crude way the Positivists suggested, the subject will all the same be essentially idle. The study of metaphysical texts may exercise our intellects and even sharpen our wits; what it cannot do, on this view of the matter, is to improve our understanding.

11

True and False in Metaphysics

1. *The attack on metaphysics as 'unscientific'*

IT IS very common today to equate 'metaphysical' with 'untestable' and hence with 'unscientific'. The pronouncements of science, it is said, have the distinguishing characteristic that they can all be brought to the test of experience; particular occurrences are relevant to the decision whether or not to accept a suggested conclusion in this field. Metaphysical theories, by contrast, are widely believed to be compatible with any state of affairs whatsoever: nothing will count decisively either for or against them. The inference that we cannot properly speak of metaphysical truth seems entirely natural.

This attack on metaphysics is perhaps less damaging than appears at first sight. Not surprisingly in view of its origins, it owes its force to acceptance of a version of Hume's Fork. The metaphysician is asked whether his propositions are tautologies or putative truths of fact; and on the assumption that he will choose the latter alternative, he is requested to show what empirical difference would be made by our accepting or rejecting what he says. But it is clear from our preceding discussions that the central contentions of metaphysicians should be represented neither as tautologies nor as pretended statements of fact. As we have seen, they are, or are closely connected with, categorial principles, whose role in knowledge is not the less genuine because it was not sufficiently noticed by the classical empiricists and their modern successors.

Categorial principles function as rules, and so cannot strictly be said to be either true or false. But to see this is to shift the problem, not to solve it. For after all we are presented in metaphysics with competing sets of first principles; we want to know which to take as correct or authentic. We could, of course, follow Collingwood and say that this question simply does not arise, for categorial principles are supposed, not asserted. But to do this would in effect be to acquiesce in the adverse verdict of the Positivists, and moreover to acquiesce prematurely, since it is by no means obvious that to treat a rule as ultimate is to accept it for no reason at all. We need to ask whether there are any rational criteria for preferring one set of metaphysical principles to another.

We also need to meet a more general version of the criticism made in our first paragraph. In mathematics, in the natural sciences and, more doubtfully, in history and the social sciences, we know, in principle at any rate, what considerations will rule out a suggested proposition as unacceptable. The type of consideration adduced varies from case to case, but there is nevertheless general agreement among those concerned in any particular instance. A scientist who has put forward a theory which has not been borne out by the facts, or a mathematician whose proposed theorem is shown to be inadequately grounded, can scarcely persist with his asseverations unchanged without damaging his professional standing. But there seems to be nothing comparable in the case of metaphysics. The same positions are taken up there over and over again; objections, however seemingly cogent, have little or no effect. General agreement on what a metaphysician would have to do to make good his case, or even to prove that an opponent is definitively in error, is conspicuously lacking. The babble of discordant voices, to echo a phrase of Hume's,[1] is as loud as it was three hundred years ago, and when we listen closely we find that much the same things are being said now as then. To take metaphysics as a serious undertaking in these circumstances seems well-nigh impossible.

2. *Agreement and disagreement in science, history and morals*

But before accepting this conclusion we should perhaps ask why there is this striking difference between metaphysics and other types of study. Why can we get clear decisions about acceptability or unacceptability in science and mathematics, and not in metaphysics?

1. Cf. Hume's introduction to the *Treatise*, p. xviii, ed. Selby-Bigge.

I suggest that part of the answer is that scientific and mathematical enquiries proceed inside a framework of presuppositions whose correctness is taken for granted by all who engage in them, whereas the whole activity of the metaphysician consists in championing one particular set of presuppositions as against others. Confronted with a problem in physics, there is a sense in which we know from the start what to think: we know at least that certain kinds of question must be asked, and that certain others are definitely inadmissible. And though it is true that fundamental assumptions in the scientific disciplines are not static, the important point here is that they are neither in a state of constant flux nor liable to change all at once. The general framework may shift, but the shift is a gradual one. What is more, the later state is not just a substitute for the earlier, but claims to develop out of it: there may be and often is resistance to change here, but to keep up resistance beyond a certain point is recognized as irrational. It is not just a case of one way of thinking being in fashion at one epoch and another at another.

No doubt this is not the whole story: the success of the sciences is due to more than their proceeding inside a framework of agreed general assumptions. The development of effective experimental techniques is obviously of immense importance, to mention only one other factor. But that agreement in fundamentals has much to do with being able to give clear decisions about what is right and what is wrong in undertakings like physics can be seen if we turn our attention to other activities where the case is perhaps not so clear. I propose to examine two such activities briefly in this connection—history and morals.

That history is a science, 'no less and no more', as J. B. Bury put it in his famous inaugural lecture at Cambridge in 1903, has been widely asserted by professional historians in the present century. It seems clear that the main ground for the claim is the conviction that historical questions are definitively decidable. In the prescientific historical era (the story goes) there was much that was arbitrary and personal in historical writing; the historical revolution which was brought to completion in the second half of the nineteenth century consisted in extruding the personal element and concentrating on the question what precisely happened, a question which historians were now in a better position to answer, thanks to the development of improved techniques for discovering and exploiting evidence. Historians must henceforth eschew any particular interest in the past and recognize that, as Ranke had put it, all periods are equally near to God. The consequence of this, according to Bury, would be the disappearance of particular 'schools' of historians and the emergence of history as an activity at once co-operative and progressive.

Reaction to these proposals on the part of subsequent historians has been significantly mixed. The great majority of academic historians in Britain were soon persuaded that Bury had made out his case: history for them had been shown to be a scientific discipline, capable of giving objective answers to the questions it posed. But there was always a small minority which remained sceptical about these claims; in America, where the influence of Continental philosophical thought about history was greater than in Britain, it was perhaps more than a small minority. And in recent years disenchantment with Bury's ideal has grown rather than diminished.[1] It has been realized increasingly that, even if some factual questions in history can be answered with certainty, this does not mean that we are in a position to give an agreed account of what happened, still less to explain it. More enters into the construction of such an account than the careful exploitation of evidence; we bring judgments of what is ultimately important in history to bear as well. Such judgments cannot be deduced from the facts: their role is rather to direct empirical enquiry, to put us on to facts we shall judge to be significant. And whilst it is the case that most professional historians in this country are agreed in their judgment of what is ultimately important in history (it is this above all which explains their general complacency), the possibility that others will take a different view can obviously not be ruled out. In countries where Marxism, or even Roman Catholicism, make a greater intellectual impact than they do in Britain, the possibility is converted into actuality, and the problem of historical objectivity becomes a live issue instead of a philosopher's pastime.

1. Compare e.g. Sir George Clark's introduction to the revised edition of the *Cambridge Modern History* (1957) and E. H. Carr's *What is History?* (1961).

I have tried to argue elsewhere[1] that there is something seriously defective in the whole notion of scientific history, conceived of as a timelessly true and impersonal account of what happened in the past. History is always a story, told by a particular person to a particular public; to understand an individual work of history we have to see it in its historical setting, and take account of the interests and valuations of both historian and potential readers. This is one reason why history is constantly being rewritten: it is not just that we know more than we did when the older histories were written, nor even that we are more sophisticated in our methods of interpretation than historians were in those days: there is the further fact that they do not ask the precise questions in which we are interested. Their outlook (a term which covers their scheme of values among other things) is in important ways different from our own, and that means that we feel it necessary to take a further look at the periods with which they deal. The very fact that this occurs is enough to cut off the historian from final truth; and when we add, with the considerations of the previous paragraph in mind, that there are available at any one time a plurality of versions of any well-known set of events (say, the Reformation or the French Revolution), scepticism about whether historical questions are definitively answerable is bound to grow. If we never quite approach the chaotic world of metaphysics here, we certainly seem to have moved some way from the orderly domain of physics.

Let us now look at a somewhat similar case, whose importance for the comparison with metaphysics will be evident, the case of morals. Here we are of course concerned not so much with assertions as with decisions, and the question we have to ask is to what extent there is an agreed procedure for reaching acceptable moral decisions. I suggest that if we try to answer this question by looking at the facts, instead of importing preconceived notions, we find that the answer varies considerably from one society and one age to another.

There have been times in the history of morals when fundamental moral disagreement was minimal: people have, broadly, accepted the same list of moral rules and thought the same types of conduct virtuous or vicious. In circumstances like these there is of course

1. See my essay 'The Limits of Scientific History', printed in *Historical Studies*, III, ed. James Hogan (London and Cork, 1961).

argument over difficult cases, just as there is in law, where the rules are also clear and the only problem is to apply them properly; but there are also many decisions which are completely uncontroversial. In extreme instances of this type of situation there is a tendency to confuse moral rules with truths of fact, and to think of the moral law as part and parcel of the natural order of things.

But there are of course wholly different moral conditions, marked by the prevalence of competing sets of moral standards and often accompanied by a widespread scepticism about whether anything is really right or wrong, good or evil; here people say that morals is nothing but a matter of convention, and often add that the conventions are introduced and enforced to suit particular interests. I think myself that it is worth stressing that even in these conditions of seeming moral chaos there remain some parts of society where the (or a) moral system continues to work: there is a tendency for people to separate themselves into individual moral sets, and to evolve and operate agreed procedures inside these. Perhaps indeed there must be some measure of overall moral agreement for a society to remain in being at all: many important items can be in dispute, but some sort of consideration for other people, some sort of dependability over undertakings are called for if the transactions of everyday life are to be carried through with any degree of success. Philosophers, like journalists, are strongly prone to exaggeration when they come to consider these matters. Yet when all allowances for exaggeration are made, it cannot be denied that there are times and societies in which we are faced with conditions of near moral breakdown. Widely divergent views about what is fundamentally desirable are maintained, and there are no generally accepted procedures for resolving such disagreement. But these are, of course, very much the conditions we meet with when we consider the question of truth in metaphysics.

The lesson to be drawn from these cases is that it is unfair to compare metaphysics with the natural sciences or mathematics in respect of their claims to truth. To repeat the main point: clear decisions about whether to accept or reject a scientific proposition are possible because science is an activity which proceeds under agreed rules, rules which, among other things, specify what is to count as evidence for or against. In metaphysics, by contrast, we are not so much working under rules as advocating them, with the result that objective proof, proof that is to say which any right-thinking person would acknowledge, is not to be had. In this context the dispute turns on what is meant by the phrase 'right-thinking person'. And that this circumstance does not immediately destroy the intellectual respectability of metaphysics is shown by the fact that we find something analogous in history, which is on any account an imporant branch of human activity, and again in morals, which is admittedly a practical undertaking but inside which there can arise very much the same controversy about fundamentals as in metaphysics.

3. *Scope and adequacy in metaphysics*

At this point we must switch to the question whether there are really no objective criteria for choosing between conflicting sets of metaphysical principles. On the face of it one such criterion seems to be obvious. We have described it as being at least part of the task of the metaphysician to give a connected account of the world as a whole. If this is accepted, it follows that one test which every metaphysical system must meet is that it should be able to cover all the facts of experience. And it may be added (as, following Professor S. C. Pepper,[1] I myself did in a previous discussion of the subject) that the 'covering' in question must give satisfaction to experts in the particular fields concerned, and not merely be adequate from the metaphysician's own point of view.

Unhappily these tests are more promising in theory than they turn out to be in practice. Take first the bare requirement to cover all the facts, and consider it with reference once more to materialism. Many people reject materialism on the ground that it brusquely dismisses whole areas of experience as illusory, but would a materialist agree that his philosophy left anything out? Suppose it were said that he failed to take account of, say, the phenomena of religious experience or the compelling character of the feeling of moral obligation. His comment would surely be that he not only mentioned these phenomena but explained them, and explained them in the only way

1. The terms 'scope' and 'adequacy' in the heading to this section are taken from Professor Pepper's book *World Hypotheses* (1942).

which could make them intelligible. In the case of religion, for example, he showed how it was, i.e. in what physical, psychological and perhaps social conditions, people came to have what are commonly called religious experiences and why they were disposed to put a certain construction on those experiences. And if it were suggested to him that this explanation simply omits what is of the essence of the matter, in so far as it says nothing about the cognitive content of such experiences, he would reply that it is an illusion to suppose that they have any such content. Having a religious experience is perhaps like being vividly aware of the presence of another person, with the difference that in this case there is no other person to be aware of. The important point, however, is that we can see how the illusion develops and what purpose it serves.

The trouble about testing a theory like that of materialism by its capacity to cover all the facts is that there is no general agreement about what 'the facts' are. Facts exist, or perhaps we should say obtain, only from particular points of view, and here points of view are in dispute. The consequence of this is that the metaphysician is necessarily judge in his own case, for though he must admit to an obligation to take account of all the facts as he sees them, it is in the last resort for him to say what is fact and what not. His office confers on him the duty of giving an overall interpretation, but simultaneously allows him a veto on accepting anything which cannot be fitted into his scheme.

It might be thought that these difficulties could be overcome if we brought in the second test mentioned above and demanded that the facts be not merely covered but covered adequately, the deciding voice on what is adequate to lie with experts in the different fields concerned. But this test too is not easy to apply. If we take the prescription literally and allow anyone with special qualifications in a particular area of human activity, say religion or natural science, to have his say, the chances are that every metaphysical theory will be turned down by somebody or other. Metaphysics will be on trial before a sort of Polish Diet, which can only give a favourable verdict in the unlikely event of its members being unanimous. Yet if alternatively we relax the requirements and allow the competing parties to pick and choose among the experts, it may well turn out that they all, or nearly all, find someone to speak in their favour. Anyone who

doubts this should reflect on the facts that the supporters of Idealism, which seems on the face of it contemptuous of scientific achievements, have always included a small number of practising scientists,
and that there are religious men who are apparently quite willing to
swallow a contemporary account of religious discourse according to
which 'God exists' means, roughly, 'Love one another'.

It would be wrong to conclude that these tests are totally useless.
In trying to assess a metaphysical theory with which we are deeply
concerned, such as materialism, we do find ourselves asking if it
covers all the facts, or again if it *really* covers them, and we are not
put off asking these questions when it is shown that they have no
generally agreed answers. What we do in situations like this is make
up our own minds as best we can, on such evidence and with such
knowledge as we can come by. Nor in point of fact is this the only
type of context in which we find ourselves forced to make a semi-
subjective judgment of this kind. The position in criticism, I mean
criticism of literature and the arts,[1] is closely similar. There too
theories are put forward and argued about with passion, but there
are no decisive tests to which appeal can be made to settle the issue
one way or the other. Considerations can be and are adduced in
support of a given interpretation or reading (I am thinking of the
different interpretations or readings which critics offer of a contro-
versial work of literature like *Hamlet*), but the weighting to be
assigned to them is a matter for personal decision. However confident he may be about the correctness of his way of taking the work,
a critic can do no more with the sceptic who persists in finding his
views unplausible than tell him to go back to the text, make an
honest effort to see it in the way recommended, and then say
whether fresh enlightenment does not result. If the answer is still
negative it is hard to see what further move could be made, for there
is no such thing as knock-down proof in this field, but only more or
less well-supported conviction.

The fact that there is no definitive procedure for rejecting a critical
theory does not show that all such theories must be arbitrarily
adopted, still less that they are totally lacking in significance. Even
the wildest critic supports his case with reasons of a sort: he hopes

1. In what follows I am primarily concerned with how to take works
of art, not with their value.

to convince others that the view he takes is correct, which is to say that it is intersubjectively valid. Nor could it be said that educated persons generally find critical argument unprofitable, despite the shortcomings we have indicated: there seems indeed to be a steady demand for this type of literature, and the evidence is that it genuinely helps the reader to make up his mind about the works on which it is a commentary. The important thing here is, however, that it is the reader who has to make a final decision: there is no such thing as a scientifically authenticated interpretation to which we are all required to subscribe whether we see anything in it or not. But that this should be so need cause no alarm, for in the field of literature and the arts understanding and experience cannot be properly divorced.

4. Metaphysical truth and critical authenticity

I suggest that the problem of metaphysical truth and metaphysical argument gains more illumination if we pay attention to activities like literary criticism than if we concentrate, as has so often been done in the past, on comparing metaphysics with the sciences or mathematics.

Admittedly this suggestion is not in line with the programmatic utterances of metaphysicians themselves, who normally present their arguments as compulsive and frequently imply that their conclusions are not merely true but necessarily true. I have already tried to show that such claims rest on a misunderstanding of the logical character of metaphysical principles, which are treated as compulsive by those who accept them but which cannot, just because they are taken as ultimate, be proved either logically or empirically.

Admittedly again there are respects in which it is easier to establish a point in criticism than in metaphysics: the former is the more circumscribed activity, and has the advantage of having fixed data in the shape of more or less well-established texts round which interpretation must centre. One of the main troubles of metaphysics, by contrast, is that there are no neutral data to which every metaphysician can be expected to do justice.

But it would be a mistake to set too much store by this difference.

We know with reasonable certainty what words Shakespeare used when he wrote *Hamlet*, but this in itself only determines to a minor degree how the play is to be taken. Philological studies can rule out some extravagances of interpretation, by showing that it is anachronistic or absurd to think that the words could bear the suggested meaning, but they cannot pronounce on how we are to see connections in the play once the literal meaning is agreed. And though other parts of the apparatus of literary scholarship—enquiries in the history of ideas, for example—are relevant to this problem, they do not in themselves suffice to resolve it. If they did, there would be no room for further critics of genius, for some literary problems would have been finally solved and others be on the way to final solution.

In assessing the work of a literary critic we look for qualities like depth, penetration, insight. We expect a good critic to reveal to us aspects of the writings under review whose significance is commonly overlooked, and so to enable us to look at what we thought we knew well with fresh eyes. It is illumination or, in a special sense of the term, understanding which we hope to derive from such a critic. But these are of course the qualities and results we associate with metaphysics, according to the argument of this book. We find a writer like Aristotle or Hegel revelatory, not because he tells us facts with which we were previously unfamiliar (though he may remind us of facts we had forgotten or overlooked), nor yet because he offers limited explanations of the scientific type, but because he enables us to take a connected view of many different kinds of facts, and in so doing to see them afresh and find in them new significance. And the procedure for authenticating a revelation of this kind is identical in the two spheres: in each case what we have to do is, first, make the interpretative principles clear, and then show that they provide genuine illumination when applied to the detailed facts. Argument can and does come in here, but in the last resort it is a matter of inviting the reader to take the principles and see for himself.

It may be thought that this comparison, if successfully sustained, shows metaphysical enquiry to be futile, since it makes everything turn on insight and personal decision. I should like to make clear that I have not wanted to argue that vision constitutes the whole, or even the major part, of metaphysics. As I tried to point out at a much earlier stage, there is a profound difference between the work of the metaphysician and that of the poet, even the philosophical poet, despite the fact that both may be said to see things in a certain way: the metaphysician is, on the lowest estimate, much the more intellectual. For this reason he needs more than the good idea and pregnant images which suffice for the poet; he has to have an idea which is articulated and can be shown to apply. And much of the activity of a metaphysician consists in elaborating a theoretical structure in accordance with a basic insight, as can be seen if we reflect in this connection on the system of Leibniz, in whose thinking concepts like *monad, perception* and *point of view* are closely linked, or that of Aristotle, where, as we have already seen, the notion of *substance* is connected with that of *nature*, and the two are spelled out in the distinctions of *matter and form* on the one hand and *potentiality and actuality* on the other. There is certainly room for objective argument about whether this work of articulation is well or ill done, though criticism will have to be offered from the inside if it is to avoid the danger of being merely verbal. And the question whether the different parts of a metaphysical system are truly coherent is also one that can be objectively determined, once the force of its various assertions has been grasped; though here again the difficulty of settling this latter point must not be underestimated.

Yet the fact remains after all this that neither 'Plato' nor 'Epicurus', to revert to Kant's curious examples,[1] can demonstrate the correctness of his metaphysical point of view: each is driven to appeal to personal testimony in support of his affirmations, and thus risks the retort, at bottom unargued, that there is nothing in what he says. It appears from this that, so far from being queen of the sciences, metaphysics cannot be a science at all. And this consequence has, in my opinion, to be accepted: we need to recognize plainly that metaphysical principles can no more be fixed in a scientific way than can moral principles. But it does not follow that principles of either sort are adopted without reason. We have mentioned already that there are circumstances—failure to cover all the facts, or to cover them adequately—in which an honest metaphysician has no choice but to abandon his principles; and whilst it is true that this is more readily recognized in theory than in practice, the pressure of the facts is even so felt in this sphere. If the reasons to which metaphysi-

1. See p. 125 above.

cians appeal do not, as they themselves suppose, necessitate, they nevertheless incline. Despite the appearances, objections to a position formulated in full consciousness of what it amounts to cannot be indefinitely shuffled off. Or if they are seemingly ignored, the ignoring is done by a succession of different persons, not by a single thinker who has dogmatically set his face against the light. An individual who feels the need to come to terms with metaphysical issues will certainly agree that such objections have to be met, and his conviction of the correctness of his own standpoint will undoubtedly be lessened if he proves unable to meet them.

A purist might say that in so far as personal judgment and decision enter into metaphysical thinking, validity and truth are shown the door. But this is to put the point much too strongly. If arguments in metaphysics necessarily differ from those we meet with in the spheres of mathematics and natural science, it does not follow that they cannot be found convincing or unconvincing. And if metaphysical assertions cannot of their nature be set down as strictly true or false, we may all the same want to characterize a set of them as illuminating or the reverse, or to describe them as authentic or spurious. These are all terms which figure in the vocabulary of criticism, and whose use there is generally accepted by those who concern themselves with literary interpretation. If it is in order in the one field, I do not see why it should not be in order in the other. And once the possibility of authenticity in metaphysics is allowed, the value of engaging in metaphysical enquiry can no longer be questioned. But the value is one which accrues to the individual, as commonly happens in the humanities; it is not, as is scientific or mathematical knowledge, the common possession of mankind as a whole.

To avert misunderstanding I should perhaps add that in making this comparison between metaphysics and criticism I have not wished to claim any privileged position for the latter. If the metaphysician is to pronounce on the scheme of things entire, he may need to say something about criticism too. Metaphysics, in fact, is an activity which is *sui generis*, and for that reason any comparison we make between it and other disciplines can be no more than partial. Yet, as we know from other cases (comparison between history and the natural sciences, for instance), resemblance does not need to be complete to be enlightening. My point about metaphysics and criticism is that they appear to be sufficiently similar for it to be worth asking whether the relative success of the one may not bear on the intellectual respectability of the other. But whether the comparison can be made out the reader must judge for himself.

5. Metaphysics and the Supersensible

It will not have escaped notice that the foregoing discussion of truth and argument in metaphysics has been conducted with exclusive reference to the type of metaphysical system which offers an overall reading of experience, the type which was called 'immanent' metaphysics earlier in this book. It remains to ask to what extent the charity I have claimed for metaphysics as so conceived can be properly extended to metaphysical theories whose connection with experience is less obvious.

As regards those systems of metaphysics which purport to transcend the range of the senses altogether and bring us news of a better world, my inclination is to follow Kant and argue that there can be no question of truth and falsity, not even in the weakened sense employed above. Systems of this sort depend, in ways I have tried to illustrate in Chapters 6 and 7, on arguments which are fundamentally faulty. You cannot build a defensible theory about the nature of things on the deliverances of pure reason, as some philosophers have tried to do, nor can you argue from immediate experience to what lies behind the veil of sense along the lines which were followed in traditional philosophy. I admit that this case has been presented no more than sketchily in the present book, but nevertheless feel that it is in essentials unassailable.

There is, however, one point here which it seems to me important to concede to transcendent metaphysicians. Positivists and others speak as if systems of this sort were and must be entirely baseless. But in fact when we reflect on the background and interests of the persons who produce such systems, we see that the practice of religion tends to play a very large part in their lives. It is from what they take, and rightly take, to be demanded in religious practice that they derive their basic conviction that the familiar world is not the only world. The worshipper must believe God to be at once a real existent (as opposed to a mere fiction) and a being who, though he reveals his presence by actions in the common world, is essentially not of it. We may say if we like that religion, in its normal forms at least, would not make sense unless this were taken to be true: to be committed to it is an important part of what we mean by religious belief. And transcendent metaphysics takes over this practical conviction, as it clearly is initially, and gives it unrestricted theoretical validity. Aside from the formal arguments he adduces, the exponent of such a system can claim that there is something in what he says just because his fundamental assumption is made in an important area of human experience.

I am not suggesting that this defence of transcendent metaphysics is sound; my point is only that it has a certain plausibility. If it is once allowed to be plausible, we cannot dismiss this sort of philosophizing out of hand, and indeed can see why it should constantly recur in the history of thought despite the derision with which sceptics have received it. We can also see what has to be done to decide if the sceptics are justified: we need to enquire whether making what Hume called the 'religious hypothesis' central will enable us to give a coherent account of the whole of experience. But this is, of course, a problem in immanent, not in transcendent, metaphysics.

This brings me to what may be called mixed systems: a theocentric metaphysics would be mixed in so far as it purported to offer an overall interpretation of experience but coupled this with the affirmation that God is the reality of realities. As we have seen, there are many metaphysical systems of this general type: Aristotle and Leibniz may be mentioned as typical authors in this genre. The difficulty, indeed, is to find examples of metaphysical theories, except perhaps in eastern philosophy, which can be called unequivocally transcendent. But this difficulty is slight compared with that of justifying the existential assertions which play such an important role in mixed systems.

An apparently easy way out of the difficulty is to claim that we know that God, or the Forms, or pure spiritual substance exist 'by intuition'. The intuiting in question will have to be done not by the bodily eyes or senses, but by what Plato called the 'eye of the soul' and Descartes the 'eye of the mind'. Various explanations are put forward by those sympathetic to this way of thinking to account for the otherwise surprising fact that this organ is unusually sensitive in some individuals and virtually non-existent in others: it is said, for instance, that preoccupation with bodily needs clouds a man's intellect, with the result that he does not 'see' what is evidently before him. Unfortunately such explanations appear to take for granted the point at issue and so can scarcely convince the sceptic. Yet in their absence the case for intellectual intuition is at best remarkably weak.

The obvious move for the believer in supersensible realities to make once the appeal to direct intuition is abandoned is to say that their existence can be inferred from what we know in experience. The difficulty here is that the things in question are supposed to be totally different in kind from anything we have met with in common life, so that inference to them from familiar facts seems impossible. You can argue from what falls within experience to what might fall within experience, but not to that which transcends experience altogether. On this point the discussions of Hume and Kant are clearly definitive.

The only remaining possibility is to say that the ontological assertions in mixed metaphysical systems cannot be taken literally, but must be interpreted in an indirect way. To say that God exists would amount in this view to saying that we should adopt a certain attitude to experience: the force of the seemingly existential assertion will come out in the consequences of accepting it, and God will be treated not as an actual existent but rather as a theoretical construct. And if the religious believer protests that this makes nonsense of the whole concept, the answer will be that we are concerned here with 'God' as a term in metaphysics, not with the God of religion.

There are, of course, many precedents in other studies for treating what look like straightforward existential statements in this way. That there are electrons is (or was) a fundamental tenet in physical theory. Yet an electron is, apparently, not the sort of thing that could be met with in experience; it is a supersensible entity not just in the sense that it is too small for our senses to discriminate, but also because it lacks characteristics which any object of sense-experience would have to possess. What kind of existence can we then ascribe to electrons? The answer would seem to be the 'ideal' existence which belongs less disputably to entities like the Freudian Censor. Nobody supposes that there literally is in each one of us a little man who suppresses some of our thoughts and turns them over to the Unconscious, even if he is otherwise disposed to accept the Freudian theory; it seems obvious that here we have to do with a mere *façon de parler*, convenient for many purposes and justified because it helps to explain otherwise puzzling facts. And the suggestion is that electrons, along with the unexperienceable entities of mixed metaphysical systems, should be thought of in the same way.

But we have still to ask whether the two cases are strictly parallel. Suppose we agree that electrons are not actual existents but theoretical constructs: the justification for giving them a place in physical theory will be that it helps to throw light on appearances and suggests fresh lines of enquiry. Moreover, the adequacy of this way of talking is in a certain way open to experimental testing: its adoption commits us to expect that things will turn out in particular ways, and its utility will be impaired if they do not. But it seems clear that no such justification can be put forward for the theoretical constructs of the metaphysician. The latter conducts no experiments and makes no discoveries, so there can be no question of justifying what he postulates by its empirical fertility. Nor could it be said that there are clear criteria, as there are supposed to be in the scientific cases, for deciding when talk in terms of, say, monads should be rejected as unilluminating. It is an old objection to metaphysicians that their theories are not open to empirical confutation. The man who builds his metaphysics round the concept of God will stick to it no matter what the facts.

I am inclined to think that this contrast is commonly drawn too sharply. Metaphysical theories are not testable in the same way as scientific theories, but then metaphysical pronouncements differ in their logical character from scientific pronouncements and are, so to speak, at a different distance from fact. It is overall understanding that the metaphysician seeks to provide, not merely understanding in a particular area, and this means that he must stand back from particular enquiries and consider their presuppositions rather than their results. But, as I have tried to argue already, this does not mean that he can afford to be indifferent to the facts in any sphere. On the contrary, what scientists discover may on occasion be of decisive

importance for him, as it is for example when the truth of materialism is in question. For reasons explained earlier in this chapter, it is
perhaps too much to hope for a really clear-cut decision in a case
like this; there is a sense in which every man has to make up his
mind on the point for himself, as it were without benefit of expert
opinion. It would, even so, be precarious to infer that judgment must
in all such cases be arbitrary: an honest man will feel the pressure of
the facts here as in the scientific sphere, and will abandon his view if
he feels that it fails to cover them. And if his view involves commitment to theoretical constructs of the kind discussed in the present
section, he will naturally abandon these too.

12

Metaphysics and Analysis

1. *Philosophy and the clarification of ideas*

Commentators on the contemporary cultural scene often draw a sharp contrast between philosophy on the European Continent and philosophy as it is practised in professional circles in Britain today, very much to the advantage of the former. Philosophy on the Continent, we are told, remains predominantly metaphysical; philosophers there are not afraid to raise, and indeed to offer answers to, large issues of concern to all thinking persons, nor do they see anything extravagant in the traditional demand that the philosopher should pronounce on the ends of life. By contrast, philosophers in Britain are alleged to restrict themselves to questions whose importance is obvious to no one but themselves, and whose bearing on other matters is minimal. They engage in what they call the analysis of concepts or discourse on linguistic usage, but their work results in nothing constructive and accordingly produces no enlightenment. Moreover, they insist that it is not their business as philosophers to offer advice on right and wrong, or good and evil; as second-order enquirers they can perhaps tell us what 'good' means, but are no better qualified than the next man to say what things are good.

I shall not presume to discuss the present state of philosophy on the Continent, but should like instead to conclude this book with some brief remarks on the general antithesis between metaphysical and analytic or critical philosophy.

Analytic philosophy[1] is the product of several forces. One of the

1. For the origins of modern analytic philosophy see J. O. Urmson: *Philosophical Analysis* (Oxford, 1956) or (for a more elementary account) *The Revolution in Philosophy* (London, 1956), by A. J. Ayer and others.

original aims of those who introduced it was to analyse facts and statements into their simplest components, and thus to make their true shape clear. Another was to make philosophy scientific, which meant in their view getting philosophers to occupy themselves with decidable questions, instead of raising large issues which there was no hope of tackling successfully. The way to do this, according to the analysts, was twofold: problems must be taken piecemeal, instead of being taken up all at once, and a technical vocabulary must be introduced to ensure that those engaged knew what they were talking about. It was in fulfilment of this programme that Russell devoted so much of his attention to the problem of perception, and in particular to the question of the relationship of immediate perceptual data to physical objects. He hoped that the possession of concepts like *sense-datum* and *logical construction* would put philosophers in a position to give a definitive solution to this problem.

Russell in his youth was averse to the traditional idea that the philosopher is a wise man; he saw him instead as a special sort of scientist. And he thought that philosophers should abstain from giving moral advice because moral questions could not be scientifically determined: no scientific procedure could decide that one way of life was better than another, for good and bad were at bottom matters of feeling. But in other respects Russell was less distant from his great predecessors than some of his followers have suggested. The programme of Logical Atomism, as we have already had occasion to remark, was a programme for saying what the world was really like (what was the underlying form of the facts, as opposed to their surface appearance), and as such was metaphysical. Nor was Russell's hankering after scientific status for the philosopher evidence of anti-metaphysical feeling, for he might have said, as his distinguished follower W. V. Quine has, that metaphysics or ontology is simply the most general form of science.

It was at a somewhat later date that the antithesis between *speculative* and *critical* philosophy, as C. D. Broad had called it in an influential essay,[1] was sharpened up and presented as absolute. Indeed, it was only in the 'thirties that it gained anything like general acceptance, and it owed its acceptance then to the spread of the

1. *Contemporary British Philosophy*, 2nd series (1925).

doctrines of Logical Positivism. The very name of this movement, as it was significantly called, proclaimed its members' antipathy to metaphysics, the supposed science of things as they really are. All possible objects of human enquiry fell, as Hume had already observed, under the twin headings of matter of fact, the province of the empirical sciences, and relations of ideas, the province of logic and mathematics. There was accordingly simply no room for a separate science of philosophy. What then could philosophers do that might be useful? The answer given was that they could clarify ideas. There were many concepts which were in daily use, by plain men or scientists or both, but whose proper analysis remained obscure. And since the lack of a clear analysis of such ideas as those of *knowledge* or *law* or *explanation* led to conceptual confusion, it could be claimed that the work of clarification was a contribution, though not perhaps a very spectacular one, to scientific advance. It must be recognized, even so, that philosophical analysis as thus understood was essentially a parasitic activity: philosophy on this reckoning was at best the handmaid of the sciences, and would have no existence or *raison d'être* apart from the latter.

This conception of philosophy as clarificatory is by no means as new as the foregoing remarks may suggest. Locke at the end of the seventeenth century had notoriously seen his task as being to act as 'under-labourer' to the great masters like Newton and Huyghens, by making clear what is involved in the notion of knowledge in particular, and analysis of this sort was henceforth a significant feature of the British way of philosophizing, being practised in the spheres of morals, aesthetics and politics as much as in that of theory of knowledge. But Locke was certainly not the first analytic philosopher. The works of Plato and Aristotle contain many brilliant examples of philosophical analysis; Aristotle's elucidation of the notions of capacity and disposition, and his application of the results to the cases of knowledge and the virtues respectively, may be mentioned as especially noteworthy. And indeed there are few, if any, philosophical writers of importance who have not seen it as at least part of their task to throw new light on ideas with which we are all more or less familiar by showing just what they come to. This is certainly as true in the cases of Hegel and Bradley as it is in those of Hume and Mill. It is, incidentally, also true of at least some notable Continental philosophers of the present day, for example Sartre.

What then is the difference between metaphysical and non-metaphysical philosophy? The answer is not that the latter is analytic and the former not, but that the latter claims to be exclusively analytic. Metaphysics having been ruled out as impossible, there is nothing left for the philosopher to do but clarify ideas. And every such piece of clarification, if the job is to be properly done, must be carried out from a standpoint which is strictly neutral: the analytic philosopher must not, as it were, put anything of himself into the analysis, but must stick to the plain task of elucidating concepts or terms as they are actually used. It follows that success or failure in any single piece of analysis will be without bearing on success or failure in another. Philosophical problems can, as Russell supposed, be tackled piecemeal, for though philosophy may have universally applicable methods, it will certainly not issue in any universal doctrine. By contrast, the analyses put forward by metaphysicians must in the nature of the case be systematically connected; they must go together to constitute an overall interpretation of experience or view of the world. And metaphysics will seem exciting by comparison with non-metaphysical philosophy, just because metaphysics tells us that things are not at all what they seem to be, whilst non-metaphysical philosophy, in the words of Wittgenstein, 'leaves everything as it is'.

Now it is not difficult to show that much of what has passed for analytic philosophy in the last thirty or forty years has been covertly metaphysical. One has only to think of all those theses which more recent philosophers have denounced as 'reductive', theses such as that of phenomenalism in the philosophy of perception, to see the force of this contention. When they announced that statements about material bodies could be replaced without loss of meaning by statements about actual or possible experiences, and again when they said that 'X was free to do y' meant nothing more than 'X could have done y, had he chosen', analytic philosophers were less innocent than they would have liked the world to suppose. Their motive, not to put too fine a point on it, was to further the cause of empiricism, and their analyses were not independent of one another, but took their shape from the circumstance that they were framed with this motive in mind. Nor was empiricism here metaphysically neutral, as can be seen from the interest its exponents showed in palpable fact on the one hand and natural science on the other, with their corresponding lack of interest in the life of the spirit.

Logical Positivism, as we can now see in retrospect, owed much of its attraction to its embodying a clear-cut view of the world, and the same feature will account for the attention which has been given to Professor Ryle's *Concept of Mind*, which also professes to offer no positive doctrine. In works like this we see that the proposal to practise what might be called pure analysis is by no means easy to carry out. But this does not show that pure analysis is an impossibility, and indeed it is in this activity that the majority of contemporary 'linguistic' philosophers in this country consider themselves to be engaged. The word 'analysis' is temporarily out of favour, doubtless because it is recognized that the Logical Analysts had definite metaphysical axes to grind, but to equate the contemporary outlook with belief in pure ('non-reductive') analysis, together with the acceptance of metaphysical neutralism, would probably not be unfair. Now I have given reasons already for thinking that metaphysical neutralism is not a tenable position: the demand for a coherent and comprehensive account of experience as a whole cannot be ruled out as impossible in principle. And though I agree that this does not in itself show that we cannot have analysis without metaphysics, I suspect even so that the analysis of the 'sixties will turn out in the end to be scarcely more innocent than was the analysis of the 'thirties. The time when analytic philosophers thought it their duty to make the world safe for science has certainly gone, but with some such philosophers at least the role which science once played has been taken over by common sense or 'ordinary language'. And even in those who are circumspect about these points there is discernible a tendency to assume without argument that everything in the world —every fact, every utterance and every activity—must necessarily be different from everything else, just as some earlier philosophers assumed without argument that everything in the world must be one. The dictum that 'Every thing is what it is, and not another thing', set by Moore on the title-page of one of the most influential philosophical works of the century, has been taken by many of Moore's successors to express a fundamental and unassailable truth. In basing their analytic work on this 'truth' it is not extravagant to suggest that they have adopted a distinctive metaphysical point of view.

Much analytic philosophy strikes the outsider as pedestrian or trivial, if not both, but it does not follow that it is really lacking in significance. One service it renders is the important one of clarifying ideas which cut across the boundaries of different disciplines or different areas of human activity, a task which has been seen as philosophical from the time of Aristotle. The Positivists were correct in claiming that unclarity about such ideas is a real obstacle to scientific advance, though they were not uniformly successful in elucidating them. And even when the analysis is performed with no such purpose in mind but rather for its own sake, it is clear that the results can possess a more general interest: they sometimes serve to refute alternative views put forward as part of a wider synthesis, and so have a metaphysical bearing in themselves. A case in point[1] is to be found in J. L. Austin's essay 'Ifs and Cans' (reprinted in his *Philosophical Papers*), which criticized sharply a fashionable way of interpreting moral language in the interests of determinism. The minuteness of Austin's analysis, and the fact that the upshot of his complicated argument is to destroy a general theory without replacing it by anything of a similar nature, must leave the aspiring metaphysician unsatisfied. But that work of this sort has an important bearing on the questions with which metaphysicians are themselves concerned could certainly not be denied.

I conclude that the prevailing contrast between speculative and critical philosophy, or if we prefer between metaphysics and analysis, is overdrawn. One can perhaps occupy oneself with problems of analysis without beating a metaphysical drum, or at least without beating one very loudly; but there is no clear dividing line between the two activities, for metaphysicians necessarily engage in analysis whilst analytic philosophers tend to make covert metaphysical assumptions. Things might be different if metaphysical neutralism were really defensible, but despite the fact that it had the support of Austin as well as Wittgenstein I cannot see that it is. The principle that if you once scratch an analyst you find a metaphysician under-

1. For a further case cf. the discussion of certain views of Ryle and Wittgenstein in Chapter 4, § 1 above.

neath has been proved true many times in the past (Hume is among the boldest and indeed the most attractive of metaphysicians), and I see no reason why it should not apply to the present and the future too.

2. *Metaphysics and practice*

We have still to discuss the point about metaphysics and the ends of life. Here we may begin by admitting that there is at least an important surface difference between metaphysical and non-metaphysical philosophers. Plato in the *Republic* declared that the great question was how men ought to live; the object of his discourse on things seen and things unseen was to produce an answer to this question. Spinoza in the *Ethics* first tried to prove that nothing exists save the one substance, God or Nature, and then went on to outline the position of human beings in the scheme of things as he saw it, all with a view to deducing how men should conduct themselves if they were to escape from bondage to the emotions and attain to true freedom. The profound bearing of practical questions on the origins of Hegel's metaphysical system has been documented at length in an earlier chapter. Yet we are sometimes told by modern philosophers that the old idea that there is an essential connection between philosophy and practice is entirely mistaken. Indeed, it is widely believed among students of philosophy in this country that there could be no such connection, since even if philosophy could establish what the world was really like nothing would follow about what was valuable. To think otherwise would be to fall into the error which Moore exposed under the name of the Naturalistic Fallacy, a contingency which, for many recent philosophers, has been little short of traumatic.

Fortunately it is not necessary to enter into the now much disputed question whether Moore was correct in seeing an absolute gulf between fact and value, since there is a sense in which he admits himself that what we take to be the case is relevant to what we think to be desirable or the reverse. In making any concrete judgment of value we need to have not merely convictions about what is ultimately worth while, but also an appreciation of the facts of the situation we face. And judgment can vary when readings of the facts vary, without its being necessary to suppose that ultimate values are in dispute. Now when metaphysicians are said to deduce conclusions about how men should conduct their lives from their doctrines about the nature of things, it may be argued that their premises comprise both statements about what is the case and assumptions about what is ultimately desirable, and that it is because they differ from the plain man about the first of these that their recommendations seem so novel and peculiar. What I am calling the assumptions are not derived from the metaphysics, but are simply presupposed as obvious. And it seems to me that this position, which clearly involves no formal fallacy, is that taken by metaphysicians when they pronounce about the good for man.

Plato, as we saw in Chapter 2, argued that the philosopher should spurn bodily pleasures and cultivate his soul, regarding earthly life as nothing more than a preparation for death. His assumption here was that any man would want what was to his ultimate benefit, and his conclusion turned on his apparently factual contentions that the essence of man is not body but soul, and that soul is immortal. We may well regard these contentions as far-fetched, but we must admit that Plato's position is entirely reasonable for anyone who takes them as established. And if it is suggested that Plato's is an unusual case, we may point out that metaphysical beliefs can make a difference to concrete moral judgments in quite ordinary cases. I once had a Roman Catholic pupil who told me that only belief in God and a future life kept him from a policy of straightforward hedonism, and who regarded his line of conduct as entirely logical in view of his conviction that these beliefs were rationally justified. The same view was taken, of course, by Archdeacon Paley at the end of the eighteenth century, and must have been accepted as correct by many believers both then and since.

The reason why metaphysical philosophers are fond of talking about how men should live whilst non-metaphysical philosophers confine their practical investigations to the analysis of value concepts is not at bottom that the former are ignorant of the Naturalistic Fallacy and the latter paralysed by fear of committing it; it is to be found rather in the fact that metaphysicians see the world in unusual lights whereas barely analytic philosophers do not. Consider the case of Spinoza in this connection. Spinoza persuaded himself that all that is belongs to a single system and that whatever happens follows necessarily from the nature of this system; human beings were, in his view, part of nature like everything else. Given these beliefs about what is the case (or, if you like, about how to take what is the case), it was entirely natural for him not only to see things in a new way, but also to draw unusual conclusions in the sphere of conduct. Since all that happens has to happen, there is no point in regretting that which is not to our particular satisfaction or in rejoicing over that which is; we have to see that good and bad are really no more than subjective notions, and realize that the only rational course is to try to understand why things turn out as they do, with a view to accepting it as inevitable. Moral praise and condemnation are alike unjustified, guilt and crime concepts for which the philosopher can have no proper use. Now although these striking conclusions do not follow exclusively from Spinoza's metaphysical beliefs, it is clear that the latter constitute an essential part of the premises on which he based them. Conversely, the modern analytic philosopher, who thinks that the whole truth about the world is already known to the man of educated common sense (the reader of the 'quality' Sunday newspapers, perhaps), is not in a position to produce original moral advice. A conservative in his view of the world, he is often a conservative in his moral outlook too.

This argument that there is a logical tie-up between metaphysical beliefs and practice will come as a surprise to some readers, for there is a generally current doctrine to the effect that metaphysical conviction, unlike conviction about everyday matter of fact, makes no practical difference. The case quoted in support of this is usually that of Bradley, who held as a metaphysician that the world is very different from what it seems to be, but was nevertheless prepared to behave as if this fact could be safely disregarded.

But to base a general conclusion about metaphysics on this single case is doubly unsatisfactory. For in the first place Bradley made clear, as Descartes and Hume had in not dissimilar circumstances before him, that what he was concerned with about time, space, causality, etc. was not their practical utility but their theoretical intelligibility; that they were practically indispensable was granted at the outset of the investigation. And secondly, though Bradley himself made few deductions of a practical nature from his metaphysics (except perhaps for his somewhat alarming remarks about 'social surgery'[1]), it is just not true that all metaphysicians have been content to remain on the same academic level. Plato and Spinoza, as we have just seen, each believed that his philosophy had practical consequences of the first importance; for both a philosopher was a man who not only knew the truth about the world but acted on it too. And theists and materialists, to take less exalted examples, alike hold beliefs about the world which can and do influence their conduct, even if they also fail to do so in some cases. That they sometimes fail is due, I suggest, not to any uncertainty about what they imply, still less to their being compatible with any action whatsoever, but rather to the fact that conduct is a matter of having skills and habits, which men continue to practise even when they abandon the theoretical basis which would make their exercise rational. But to show that people sometimes behave in ways which do not square with their metaphysical professions is not to prove that nobody believes professions of this sort, nor yet that such professions have no practical consequences. If it is possible to be inconsistent, it must be possible to be consistent as well.

1. 'Some remarks on punishment', *Collected Essays*, I, pp. 152 ff.

Bibliographical Note

I *Classical metaphysical writings*

The following are the main works discussed or referred to in the text:
Plato: *Phaedo, Republic, Theaetetus,* Seventh Letter
Aristotle: *Categories, Physics* (especially Book II), *Metaphysics* (especially Books Z, H, Λ)
Aquinas: *Summa theologica*
Descartes: *Discourse on Method; Meditations on First Philosophy*
Spinoza: *Ethics*
Leibniz: *Discourse on Metaphysics;* Correspondence with Arnauld; *Monadology*
Hume: *Treatise of Human Nature*
Kant: *Critique of Pure Reason*
Hegel: *Early Theological Writings; Phenomenology of Spirit*
Bradley: *Appearance and Reality*

II *Modern discussions of metaphysics*

Among the most important of these are:
C. D. Broad: 'Critical and Speculative Philosophy' in *Contemporary British Philosophy,* first series, 1924
R. Carnap: 'The Elimination of Metaphysics through Logical Analysis of Language', first published in German 1932; E. T. in A. J. Ayer (ed.), *Logical Positivism,* Glencoe, Ill., 1959
A. J. Ayer: *Language, Truth and Logic,* 1936; see also second edition introduction, 1945
R. G. Collingwood: *An Essay on Metaphysics,* 1940
D. M. Emmet: *The Nature of Metaphysical Thinking,* 1945
D. F. Pears (ed.): *The Nature of Metaphysics,* 1957

Index

A

Absolute, the, 56, 71, 75–6, 164
Absurdity (sense and nonsense), 67, 80–1, 155 ff., 165–6
Adequacy, as a criterion in metaphysics, 177–9
Analogical argument, 170
Analysis, analytic philosophy, 16, 17, 113, 153, 189 ff.
Appearance, see s.v. 'reality'
Aquinas, St Thomas, 12, 17, 37, 56, 98, 164
Argument, nature of metaphysical, 166–70, 180–4
Aristotle, 12, 17, 37, 45, 55–62, 65, 68–70, 71, 81, 84, 86–7, 97, 121–2, 161, 165, 166, 168, 169, 181, 182, 185, 191, 194
Assertions, metaphysical, 164–6
Austin, J. L., 194
Authenticity, 181–3
Ayer, A. J., 90, 189

B

Baumgarten, A., 38
Behaviourism, 51–2

Being: Becoming, Platonic contrast of, 21 ff., 46
Belief, Plato's concept of, 20–4
Berkeley, G., 66, 84
Boehme, J., 152
Bosanquet, B., 168
Bradley, F. H., 17, 45, 71, 73–7, 82, 84, 95, 111, 113, 115, 117–18, 121–2, 130, 145, 151, 191, 197
Broad, C. D., 190
Burke, E., 13, 16, 123, 130–2

C

Carnap, R., 112
Categories, categorial principles, 40, 159, 160–6, 169
Cause, Aristotle on, 58–9; Hume on 99 ff.; and sign, 100, 101; and condition, 100, 101–2; as a practical notion, 100–2, 105; and theoretical understanding, 102, 105; and metaphysics, 40, 106–8; cf. 'First Cause'
Certainty, claimed for metaphysical statements, 11, 35–6, 94–5, 165–6, 168–9, 180